Implementing DevOps with Ansible 2

Build, develop, test, deploy, and monitor in seconds

Jonathan McAllister

BIRMINGHAM - MUMBAI

Implementing DevOps with Ansible 2

First published: July 2017

Production reference: 1200717

Published by Packt Publishing Ltd.
Livery Place
35 Livery Street
Birmingham
B3 2PB, UK.

ISBN 978-1-78712-053-2

www.packtpub.com

Credits

Author
Jonathan McAllister

Reviewer
Matthew Fisher

Acquisition Editor
Meeta Rajani

Content Development Editor
Sharon Raj

Technical Editor
Vishal Kamal Mewada

Copy Editors
Madhusudan Uchil
Stuti Srivastava

Project Coordinator
Virginia Dias

Proofreader
Safis Editing

Indexer
Aishwarya Gangawane

Graphics
Kirk D'Penha

Production Coordinator
Aparna Bhagat

About the Author

Jonathan McAllister has been creating software and automations since he was a child. As an avid computer technologist, he has had 13 years of professional experience in software development, testing, and delivery practices. During his career, he has architected and implemented software build, testing, and delivery solutions for cutting-edge technology organizations across diverse technology stacks. Jonathan has most recently been focusing on build pipelines, Continuous Integration, Continuous Delivery, microservice architecture, standardized processes, Agile and Kanban, and the implementation of highly scalable automation solutions. He has worked and consulted for some of the industry's most notable companies, including Microsoft, Merck, Logitech, and Oracle.

His focus is entirely on designing scalable software build, delivery, and testing pipelines in an effort to streamline releases through standardization and help develop strategies that can elevate revenue through modern continuous practices.

Acknowledgments

This book wouldn't have been possible if it hadn't been for the support of my family, friends, previous managers and co-workers. I'd like to thank the following people for their love and support in writing this:

Family and friends:

- Stephanie Kellogg – My wife and best friend.
- Renae Pittman – My sister and one of the only people I let yell at me.
- Adrian McAllister – My son.
- Richard Vasquez – My father.
- Caden McAllister – My son.
- Trisiann Vasquez – My aunt.
- Devin McAllister – My son.
- Toni Null – My mother.
- Kailey McAllister – My dearest princess.
- Carla Muniz – My Tia.
- Bryce McAllister – My son.
- Lauren Jones – She's stuck by me for I don't know how many years. Amazing mother and friend.

Co-workers and management:

- Chris Hemphill – First taught me the constructs of SCM and Continuous Delivery.
- David Mueller – One of the best working leaders I've ever met.
- Shane McDougal – The sharpest Agile guru on the planet.
- Arsalan Baig – The most amazing designer I've ever met.
- Jonathan Krautter – Security excellence and overall security GOD!
- Charles Williams – One of the first people to mentor me and amazing human.

"Let's work to make the world a better place to be. A unified world where we can see that love is the magic that sets us free"

– Jonathan McAllister

About the Reviewer

Matthew Fisher has worked as a software developer for over 17 years in roles ranging from the Unix kernel to mobile phone development to DevOps. Matt has a passion for IT transformation projects—especially automation, self-service infrastructure, and the cloud. Matt was a contributing author on *Common OpenStack Deployments: Real-World Examples for Systems Administrators and Engineers* and has given many presentations on automating IT and deploying OpenStack. When not doing cool DevOps stuff, Matt enjoys hiking, camping, skiing, craft beer, and spending time with his family in Fort Collins, Colorado.

www.PacktPub.com

For support files and downloads related to your book, please visit `www.PacktPub.com`.

Did you know that Packt offers eBook versions of every book published, with PDF and ePub files available? You can upgrade to the eBook version at `www.PacktPub.com` and as a print book customer, you are entitled to a discount on the eBook copy.

Get in touch with us at `service@packtpub.com` for more details. At `www.PacktPub.com`, you can also read a collection of free technical articles, sign up for a range of free newsletters and receive exclusive discounts and offers on Packt books and eBooks.

`https://www.packtpub.com/mapt`

Get the most in-demand software skills with Mapt. Mapt gives you full access to all Packt books and video courses, as well as industry-leading tools to help you plan your personal development and advance your career.

Why subscribe?

- Fully searchable across every book published by Packt
- Copy and paste, print, and bookmark content
- On demand and accessible via a web browser

Customer Feedback

Thanks for purchasing this Packt book. At Packt, quality is at the heart of our editorial process. To help us improve, please leave us an honest review on this book's Amazon page at `https://www.amazon.com/dp/1787120538`.

If you'd like to join our team of regular reviewers, you can e-mail us at `customerreviews@packtpub.com`. We award our regular reviewers with free eBooks and videos in exchange for their valuable feedback. Help us be relentless in improving our products!

Table of Contents

Preface

Ansible has taken the DevOps world by storm. Its highly scalable architecture and modular implementation have made it an ideal tool for implementing DevOps solutions at organizations large and small. Implementing DevOps with Ansible 2 will provide detailed tutorials and information on how to implement DevOps solutions at your organization.Implementing DevOps with Ansible 2 aims to help encourage good software development and delivery practices within organizations by educating you on both the practical technology side of DevOps implementations as well as the cultural and collaborative implementations.Throughout the course of this book, we walk through many examples and solutions for common DevOps implementation shortcomings and automation requirements. The book walks you step by step through the implementation of solutions using examples that are easy to read and follow and simple to understand.As the author of Implementing DevOps with Ansible 2, it is my sincerest hope that this book helps you in your quest to become more DevOps and Ansible proficient. As such, I have set up a website to help readers further their knowledge and reach out to me for any questions. The URL is `http://www.ansibledevops.com`.

What this book covers

`Chapter 1`, *DevOps Fundamentals*, introduces you to DevOps (a hybrid word connecting development and operations) and educates you on the DevOps movement and how DevOps has in recent years revolutionized software development and delivery at organizations around the globe.

`Chapter 2`, *Configuration Management Essentials*, will teach you how tools like Ansible can make developers, testers, and operations work easier by eliminating environment drift, automating the provisioning of infrastructure, and providing an easy and consistent way to spin up bug reproduction environments.

`Chapter 3`, *Installing, Configuring, and Running Ansible*, will educate you on where to get Ansible, how to install and set up a control server, how to authorize the control server with inventory items and how to use the Ansible command line to run a playbook or query an infrastructure group. Finally, the chapter will educate you on the core module set and how this provide an interactive interface to other technologies (Git, JIRA, Jenkins, and so on).

`Chapter 4`, *Playbooks and Inventory Files*, will further your knowledge on playbooks, playbook trees, roles, tasks, and inventory files. In this chapter, the reader will see some basic examples of simple playbooks and learn some of the various ways to run them.

`Chapter 5`, *Playbooks: Beyond the Fundamentals*, will help you learn the syntax requirements of the YAML markup language. Additionally, the chapter will educate you on the Ansible specific syntax for roles, includes, variables, loops, blocks, conditionals, registers, and facts.

`Chapter 6`, *Jinja in Ansible*, will dive into Jinja2 templating and how to make use of it in Ansible.

`Chapter 7`, *Ansible Vault*, will outline the Ansible way of managing and deploying sensitive information and how to best leverage the Ansible Vault utility to ensure sensitive data is kept secret. You will learn (by example) how to best control and manage highly secure information and learn the underpinnings of how Ansible keeps your information secure.

`Chapter 8`, *Ansible Modules and Libraries*, will focus on the wide array of modules provided by the Ansible solution. Modules in Ansible provide the ability for playbooks to connect to and control third party technologies (some open source, some closed source). In this chapter, we will discuss the most popular ones and dive into creating playbook tasks that help manage a suite of tools and services available to developers, testers, and operators.

`Chapter 9`, *Integrating Ansible with CI and CD Solutions*, we will teach you how to leverage other DevOps related tools to control Ansible. The specific topics covered will be Jenkins and TeamCity. The reader will learn how Ansible can be leveraged as a post build action, how Ansible fits into a Continuous Integration and Continuous Delivery pipeline, and some examples for each.

`Chapter 10`, *Ansible and Docker*, we will educate you on how to use Python to extend Ansible and create custom modules that integrate with unique specific technology stacks. This will be done by providing a set of tutorials that teach the reader to write and release custom Ansible modules. The chapter will teach you how to read input, manage facts, perform automated tasks, interact with REST APIs and generate documentation.

`Chapter 11`, *Extending Ansible*, will help you learn the popular features of both Galaxy and Tower and how to use and configure both. Upon completing this chapter, you will have the knowledge needed to act as an authority in your organization for both of the unique and vibrant technologies.

`Chapter 12`, *Ansible Galaxy*, will teach how to provision Docker containers using Ansible, how to integrate Ansible with Docker's service, how to manage Docker image facts, and how to gain full control over Docker images.

What you need for this book

This book was written with Ubuntu used for the control server and SSH access to target servers. As such you will need an Ubuntu machine or VM to use the tutorials within this book. For the module and plugin creation chapter you will need Python on the Ubuntu system.

Who this book is for

This book is for anyone who is curious about DevOps implementations and how to leverage Ansible to create automated solutions.

Conventions

In this book, you will find a number of text styles that distinguish between different kinds of information. Here are some examples of these styles and an explanation of their meaning. Code words in the text, database table names, folder names, filenames, file extensions, pathnames, dummy URLs, user input, and Twitter handles are shown as follows: "If SSH key sharing is not available Ansible also offers the option to ask for a password using the `--ask-become-pass` command-line argument."

A block of code is set as follows:

```
# File name: hellodevopsworld.yml
---
- hosts: all
  tasks:
  - shell: echo "hello DevOps world"
```

When we wish to draw your attention to a particular part of a code block, the relevant lines or items are set in bold:

```
[databaseservers]
mydbserver105.example.org
mydbserver205.example.org
[webservers]
mywbserver105.example.org
mywbserver205.example.org
```

Any command-line input or output is written as follows:

```
$ sudo apt-get install software-properties-common
$ sudo apt-add-repository ppa:ansible/ansible
$ sudo apt-get update
$ sudo apt-get install ansible
```

New terms and **important words** are shown in bold. Words that you see on the screen, for example, in menus or dialog boxes, appear in the text like this: "To install the Ansible plugin. simply navigate to **Plugin Manager** (as a Jenkins administrator) and select **Ansible plugin** from the **Available** plugins tab and install the plugin."

 Warnings or important notes appear in a box like this.

 Tips and tricks appear like this.

Reader feedback

Feedback from our readers is always welcome. Let us know what you think about this book-what you liked or disliked. Reader feedback is important for us as it helps us develop titles that you will really get the most out of. To send us general feedback, simply email feedback@packtpub.com, and mention the book's title in the subject of your message. If there is a topic that you have expertise in and you are interested in either writing or contributing to a book, see our author guide at www.packtpub.com/authors.

Customer support

Now that you are the proud owner of a Packt book, we have a number of things to help you to get the most from your purchase.

Downloading the example code

You can download the example code files for this book from your account at `http://www.packtpub.com`. If you purchased this book elsewhere, you can visit `http://www.packtpub.com/support` and register to have the files e-mailed directly to you. You can download the code files by following these steps:

1. Log in or register to our website using your e-mail address and password.
2. Hover the mouse pointer on the **SUPPORT** tab at the top.
3. Click on **Code Downloads & Errata**.
4. Enter the name of the book in the **Search** box.
5. Select the book for which you're looking to download the code files.
6. Choose from the drop-down menu where you purchased this book from.
7. Click on **Code Download**.

Once the file is downloaded, please make sure that you unzip or extract the folder using the latest version of:

- WinRAR / 7-Zip for Windows
- Zipeg / iZip / UnRarX for Mac
- 7-Zip / PeaZip for Linux

The code bundle for the book is also hosted on GitHub at `https://github.com/PacktPublishing/Implementing-DevOps-with-Ansible-2`. We also have other code bundles from our rich catalog of books and videos available at `https://github.com/PacktPublishing/`. Check them out!

Downloading the color images of this book

We also provide you with a PDF file that has color images of the screenshots/diagrams used in this book. The color images will help you better understand the changes in the output. You can download this file from `https://www.packtpub.com/sites/default/files/downloads/ImplementingDevOpswithAnsible2_ColorImages.pdf`.

Errata

Although we have taken every care to ensure the accuracy of our content, mistakes do happen. If you find a mistake in one of our books-maybe a mistake in the text or the code-we would be grateful if you could report this to us. By doing so, you can save other readers from frustration and help us improve subsequent versions of this book. If you find any errata, please report them by visiting http://www.packtpub.com/submit-errata, selecting your book, clicking on the **Errata Submission Form** link, and entering the details of your errata. Once your errata are verified, your submission will be accepted and the errata will be uploaded to our website or added to any list of existing errata under the Errata section of that title. To view the previously submitted errata, go to https://www.packtpub.com/books/content/support and enter the name of the book in the search field. The required information will appear under the **Errata** section.

Piracy

Piracy of copyrighted material on the Internet is an ongoing problem across all media. At Packt, we take the protection of our copyright and licenses very seriously. If you come across any illegal copies of our works in any form on the Internet, please provide us with the location address or website name immediately so that we can pursue a remedy. Please contact us at copyright@packtpub.com with a link to the suspected pirated material. We appreciate your help in protecting our authors and our ability to bring you valuable content.

Questions

If you have a problem with any aspect of this book, you can contact us at questions@packtpub.com, and we will do our best to address the problem.

1
DevOps Fundamentals

The DevOps movement, agile development, **Continuous Integration (CI)** and **Continuous Delivery (CD)** have all played a role in reshaping the landscape of software engineering efforts throughout the world. Gone are the days of manual environment provisioning, a priesthood of release engineering, and late-night stale-pizza release parties. While the pizza may have been a highlight, it was hardly worth the 4am deployment nightmares. These now antiquated practices have been replaced with highly efficient delivery pipelines, scalable microservice architectures, and IaC automated configuration-management techniques. As a result of these innovations, a new demand for automation engineers, configuration-management personnel, and DevOps-oriented engineers has cropped up. This new demand for an engineering resource capable of both driving efficient development practices, automating configuration management, and implementing scalable software delivery has completely transformed the modern software organization.

In software engineering, the term DevOps is as equally diverse as it is popular. A simple Google search for the term `DevOps` yields roughly 18 million unique page results (that's a lot!). A search on Indeed.com for the term DevOps provides a diverse set of industry implementations. As with most culture-oriented terms, there is a buzzword definition and a deeper technical scope for the term DevOps. For the outsider, DevOps may seem a bit ambiguous. For this reason, it is often confused by organizations as an operations person who can code, or a developer who acts as an operational resource. This misnomer known as a DevOps engineer has led to significant confusion. Neither of the above provided definitions is 100% accurate.

In this book, we will add clarity to the practices surrounding the implementation of DevOps and provide you with the knowledge you will need to become both a successful DevOps and Ansible expert in your organization. In this book we will explore Ansible implementations and learn how it ties into DevOps solutions and processes. We will journey together through the Ansible and DevOps world and see how to leverage it for scalable deployments, configuration management, and automation. We will take this journey together and explore the exciting world of DevOps in Ansible 2 together. Let's get started!

In this first chapter, we are going to dive into DevOps and its methodology constructs to cover the following topics:

- DevOps 101
- The History of DevOps
- DevOps in the modern software organization
- The DevOps assembly line
- DevOps architectures and patterns

DevOps 101

In the years leading up to the 2009 DevOpsDays conference tour, the term "DevOps" was relatively unknown to the engineering and technology stratosphere. The inception of DevOps-oriented culture was provided by Patrick Debois at an agile infrastructure conference in 2008. During this conference, Patrick spoke of a highly collaborative development team he worked with during his tenure at a large enterprise. The most highly collaborative moments during this tenure were when there were site outages or emergencies. During these incidents, the developers and operations people seemed to be laser-focused and worked incredibly well together. This experience gave Patrick a yearning to encourage this behavior outside of non-emergency activities.

It was at the agile infrastructure conference that Pattick Debois was able to also connect with Andrew Shafer (who then worked at Puppet Labs, Inc.). These two soon found out that they shared many of the same goals and ideologies. In many senses, this chance encounter encouraged Patrick to continue to push the fledgling concept of DevOps forward. In future conferences, Patrick tried fervently yet unsuccessfully (at agile infrastructure conferences) to encourage a more collaborative approach to software development and delivery. While the idea was novel, the practical implementation of the idea never seemed to gain traction at the venues provided to Patrick.

It was in 2009 that Patrick Debois attended an O'Reilly *Velocity* conference, where he heard John Allspaw speak of how Ops and Dev could collaborate. From this speech, the idea of DevOps was seeded in his mind. Patrick decided to begin hosting a set of mini DevOpsDays conferences, which would eventually catapult the concept of DevOps into mainstream engineering cultures.

While there is yet to be a concise, one-line summary of everything that DevOps entails, there has come about a generally accepted agreement on the overarching concepts and practices that define DevOps: culture, automation, measurement, and sharing, or **CAMS** for short. The CAMS approach to DevOps was defined by Damon Edwards and John Willis at DevOpsDays in 2010. It is described in greater detail next.

Culture

One of the generally accepted concepts to arise out of the DevOps movement is a cultural one. With traditional IT organization being isolated from development, **silos** are a commonplace within organizations worldwide. In an effort to pave the way for rapid development and delivery, a fundamental change in organizational culture must take place. This would be done in an effort to promote collaboration, sharing, and a sense of synergy within the organization. This cultural change is indeed probably the most difficult aspect of a DevOps adoption in an organization.

Automation

Automating once-manual processes is critical for a successful DevOps transformation. Automation removes the guesswork and magic out of building, testing, and delivering software and enforces the codification of software processes. Automation is also among the more visible aspects of DevOps and provides one of the highest **returns on investment (ROIs)**.

Measurement

Measuring successes and failures provides critical business data and helps pave the way for higher efficiency through effective change. This simply emphasizes that business decisions can be made through data and metrics rather than gut reactions. For a DevOps transformation to be a success, measuring things such as throughput, downtime, rollback frequency, latency, and other related operational statistics can help pivot an organization toward higher efficiency and automation.

Sharing

In stark contrast to the previously accepted paradigm of software development, sharing is pivotal for a successful DevOps transformation. This means that teams should be encouraged to share code, concepts, practices, processes, and resources. A successful DevOps-oriented organization may even go so far as to embed an operations employees or QA resource in the development team in order to facilitate autonomy and collaborative teams. Some organizations may also have shared or overlapping roles. This may be realized through some modern development techniques (TDD, BDD and so on).

At the time of writing, there are hundreds if not thousands of DevOps-specific tools. Such tools are designed to make the lives of engineering organizations better or more efficient. While the tools aspect of DevOps is important, it is important to not let a given tool define your specific organization's DevOps process for you. Once again this implementation CANNOT be achieved without applying the CAMS model first. Throughout the course of this book, we will reference and tutorialize an array of different tools and technologies. For you, specifically, it's important that you select and leverage the right tool for the right job.

The History of DevOps

Prior to the widespread adoption of DevOps, organizations would often commit to developing and delivering a software system within a specified time frame and, more often than not, miss release deadlines. The failure to meet required deadlines put additional strains on organizations financially and often meant that the business would bleed financial capital. Release deadlines in software organizations are missed for any number of reasons, but some of the most common are listed here:

- The time needed to complete pure development efforts
- The amount of effort involved in integrating disparate components into a working software title
- The number of quality issues identified by the testing team
- Failed deployments of software or failed installations onto customers' machines

The amount of extra effort (and money) required to complete a software title (beyond its originally scheduled release date) sometimes even drains company coffers so much it forces the organization into bankruptcy. Companies such as Epic MegaGames or Apogee were once at the top of their industry but quickly faltered and eventually faded into the background of failed businesses and dead software titles as a result of missed release dates and a failure to compete.

The primary risk of this era was not so much in the amount of time engineering would often take to create a title, but instead in the amount of time it would take to integrate, test, and release a software title after initial development was completed. Once the initial development of a software title was completed, there were oftentimes long integration cycles coupled with complex quality-assurance measures. As a result of the quality issues identified, major rework would need to be performed before the software title was adequately defect-free and releasable. Eventually, the releases were replicated onto disk or CD and shipped to customers.

Some of the side-effects of this paradigm were that during development, integration, quality assurance, or pre release periods, the software organization would not be able to capitalize on the software, and the business was often kept in the dark on progress. This inherently created a significant amount of risk, which could result in the insolvency of the business. With software engineering risks at an all-time high and businesses averse to Vegas-style gambling, something needed to be done.

In an effort for businesses to codify the development, integration, testing, and release steps, companies strategized and created the **software development life cycle** (**SDLC**). The SDLC provided a basic outline process flow, which engineering would follow in an effort understand the current status of an under-construction software title. These process steps included the following:

- Requirements gathering
- Design
- Development
- Testing
- Deployment
- Operations

The process steps in the SDLC were found to be cyclic in nature, meaning that once a given software title was released, the next iteration (including bug fixes, patches, and so on) was planned, and the SDLC would be restarted. In the 90s, this meant a revision in the version number, major reworks of features, bug fixes, added enhancements, a new integration cycle, quality assurance cycle, and eventually a reprint of CDs or disks. From this process, the modern SDLC was born.

An illustration of the SDLC is provided next:

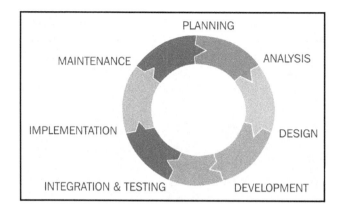

Through the creation and codification of the SDLC, businesses now had an effective way to manage the software creation and release process. While this process properly identified a repeatable software process, it did not mitigate the risk of integrating it. The major problem with the integration phase was in the risk of merging. During the time period before DevOps, CI, CD, and agile, software marching orders would traditionally be divided among teams, and individual developers would retreat to their workstations and code. They would progress in their development efforts in relative isolation until everyone was done and a subsequent integration phase of development took place.

During the integration phase, individual working copies were cobbled together to eventually form one cohesive and operational software title. At the time, the integration phase posed the most amount of risk to a business, as this phase could take as long as (or longer than) the process of creating the software title itself. During this period, engineering resources were expensive and the risk of failure was at its highest; a better solution was needed.

The risk of the integration phase to businesses was oftentimes very high, and a unique approach was finally identified by a few software pundits, which would ultimately pave the way for the future. Continuous Integration is a development practice where developers can merge their local workstation development changes incrementally (and very frequently) into a shared source-control mainline. In a CI environment, basic automation would typically be created to validate each incremental change and ensure nothing was inadvertently broken or didn't work. In the unfortunate event something broke, the developer could easily fix it or revert the change. The idea of continuously merging contributions meant that organizations would no longer need an integration phase, and QA could begin to take place as the software was developed.

Continuous Integration would eventually be popularized through successful mainstream software-engineering implementations and through the tireless efforts of Kent Beck and Martin Fowler. These two industry pundits successfully scaled basic continuous-integration techniques during their tenure at the Chrysler corporation in the mid 90s. As a result of their successful litmus tests through their new CI solution, they noticed an elimination of risk to the business via the integration phase. As a result, they eagerly touted the newfound methodology as the way of the future. Not too long after CI began to gain visibility, other software organizations began to take notice of it and also successfully applied the core techniques.

Strides toward the future

By the late 90s and early 2000s, Continuous Integration was in full swing. Software engineering teams were clamoring to integrate more frequently and verify changes faster, and they diligently worked to develop releasable software incrementally. In many ways, this was the golden era of engineering. It was at the height of the Continuous Integration revolution that (in 2001) 12 software engineering pundits met in a retreat at a mountain resort in Snowbird, Utah, to discuss a new approach to software development. The result of this meeting of the minds, known now as **agile development**, is broken down into four central pillars, which are:

- Individuals and interactions over processes and tools
- Working software over comprehensive documentation
- Customer collaboration over contract negotiation
- Responding to change over following a plan

That is, while there is value in the items on the right, we value the items on the left more.

This set of simple principles combined with the 12 core philosophies of agile development would later become known as the agile manifesto. The complete agile manifesto can be found at `http://agilemanifesto.org/`.

In 2001, the agile manifesto was officially published, and organizations soon began breaking work into smaller chunks and getting orders standing up instead of sitting down. Functionality was prioritized, and work items were divided across team members for completion. This meant that the team now had rigid timelines and 2- to 4-week deliverable deadlines.

While this was a step in the right direction, it was limited to the scope of the development group alone. Once the software system was handed from development to quality assurance, the development team would often remain hands off as the software eventually made its way to a release. The most notable problem in this era was related to large complex deployments into physical infrastructure by people who had little to no understanding of the way the software worked.

As software organizations evolved, so did the other departments. For example, **quality assurance (QA)** practices became more modern and automated. Programmers began writing automated test suites and worked to validate software changes in an automated way. From the revolution in QA, modern practices such as **Test-driven Development (TDD)**, **Behavior-driven Development (BDD)**, and **A/B Testing** evolved.

The agile movement came about in the year 2001 with the signing and release of the agile manifesto. The principles identified in the agile manifesto in many ways identified a lot of the core concepts that the DevOps movement has since adopted and extended. The agile manifesto represented a radical shift in development patterns when it was released. It argued for shorter iterative development cycles, rapid feedback, and higher levels of collaboration. Sound familiar?

It was also about this time that Continuous Integration began to take root in software organizations and engineers began to take notice of broken builds, failed unit tests, and release engineering.

DevOps in the Modern Software Organization

The solution to the issue of silos in an organization, it would seem, was to alter the culture, simplify and automate the delivery of software changes (by doing it more often), change the architecture of software solutions (away from monoliths), and pave the way for the organization to outmaneuver the competition through synergy, agility, and velocity. The idea is that if a business can deliver features that customers want faster than the competition, they will outdo their opponents.

It was for these reasons that modern DevOps approaches came to fruition. This approach also allowed incremental approaches to DevOps adoption within an organization.

The DevOps assembly line

In the infancy of computer science, computer programmers were wizards, their code was a black art, and organizations paid hefty sums to develop and release software. Oftentimes, software projects would falter and companies would go bankrupt attempting to release a software title to the market. Computer science back then was very risky and entailed long development cycles with painful integration periods and oftentimes failed releases.

In the mid 2000's Cloud computing took the world by storm. The idea of an elastic implementation of computing resources, which could scale at ease with organizations that were expanding rapidly provided a wave for the innovation of the future. By 2012 Cloud computing was a huge trend and hundreds if not thousands of companies were clamoring to get to the cloud.

As software engineering matured in the early 2000s and the widespread use of computers grew, a new software paradigm came to fruition; it was called **Software as a Service (SaaS)**. In the past, software was shipped to customers either on CD, floppy disk, or direct onsite installations. This widely accepted pricing model was in the form of a one-time purchase. This new platform provided a subscription-based revenue model and touted an elastic and highly scalable infrastructure with promises of recurring revenue for businesses. It was known as the **cloud**.

With cloud computing on the rise and the software use paradigm changing dramatically, the previously accepted big bang 5 release strategy began to become antiquated. As a result of the shifting mentality in software releases, organizations could no longer wait over a year for an integration cycle to take place prior to the execution of quality assurance test plans. Nor could the business wait two years for engineering and QA to sign off on a given release. To help solve this issue, Continuous Integration was born, and the beginnings of an assembly-line system for software development began to take shape. The point of DevOps was more than just a collaborative edge within teams. The premise was in fact a business strategy to get features into customers hands more efficiently through DevOps cultural implementations.

Correlations between a DevOps assembly line and manufacturing

Prior to the Industrial Revolution, goods were mostly handcrafted and developed in small quantities. This approach limited the quantity a craftsman could create as well as the customer base they could sell their goods to. This process of handcrafting goods proved to be expensive, time-consuming, and wasteful. When Henry Ford began developing the automobile, he looked to identify a more efficient method of manufacturing goods. The result of his quest was to implement a standardization methodology and adopt a progressive assembly-line approach for developing automobiles.

In the 1980s and 90s, software engineering efforts would oftentimes drain company finances. This was the result of inefficiencies in processes, poor communication, a lack of coordinated development efforts, and an inadequate release process. Inefficiencies such as integration phases, manual quality assurance, verification release plans, and execution often added a significant amount of time to the overall development and release strategies of the business. As a way to begin mitigating these risks, new practices and processes began to take shape.

As a result of these trends, software organizations began to apply manufacturing techniques to software engineering. One of the more prevalent manufacturing concepts to be applied to software development teams is the manufacturing assembly line (also known as **progressive assembly**). In factories all around the world, factory assembly lines have helped organize product-creation processes and have helped ensure that, prior to shipping and delivery, manufactured goods are carefully assembled and verified. The assembly-line approach provides a level of repeatability and quantifiable verification for mass-produced products. Factories adopt the progressive assembly approach to minimize waste, maximize efficiency, and deliver products of higher quality. In recent years, software engineering organizations have begun to gravitate towards this progressive assembly-line practice to also help reduce waste, improve throughput, and release products of higher quality. From this approach, the overarching DevOps concept was born.

DevOps architectures and practices

From the DevOps movement, a set of software architectural patterns and practices have become increasingly popular. The primary logic behind the development of these architectural patterns and practices is derived from the need for scalability, no-downtime deployments, and minimizing negative customer reactions to upgrades and releases. Some of these you may have heard of (microservices), while others may be a bit vague (blue-green deployments).

In this section, we will outline some of the more popular architectures and practices to evolve from the DevOps movement and learn how they are being leveraged to provide flexibility and velocity at organizations worldwide.

Encapsulated software development

In software development, encapsulation often means different things to different people. In the context of the DevOps architecture, it simply means modularity. This is an important implementation requirement for DevOps organizations because it provides a way for components to be updated and replaced individually. Modular software is easier to develop, maintain, and upgrade than monolithic software. This applies both to the grand architectural approach as well as at the object level in object-oriented programming. If you have ever worked at a software organization that has monolithic legacy code base, you are probably quite familiar with spaghetti code or the monolithic fractal Onion Software approach. Below is a monolithic software architecture vs encapsulated architecture approach diagram:

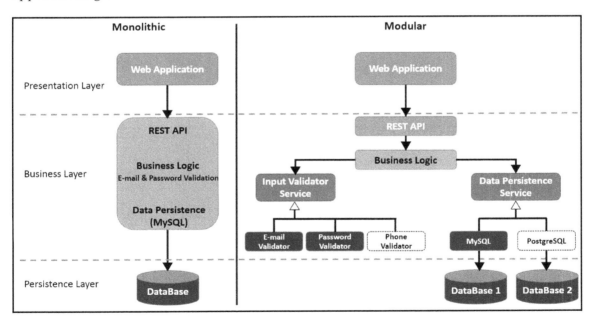

As we can see from the above diagram, the modular organized software solution is significantly easier to understand and potentially manage than the monolithic one.

Microservices

Microservices architectures cropped up around the same time as containerization and portable virtualization. The general concept behind a microservice architecture is to architect a software system in such a way that large development groups have a simplistic way to update software through repeatable deployments, and upgrade only the parts that have changed. In some ways, microservices provide a basic constraint and solution to development sprawl to ensure that software components don't become monolithic. The general practice of upgrading only the parts that have changed might be to think of this as replacing the tires on a car instead of replacing the entire car every time the tires become worn.

A microservice development paradigm requires discipline from development personnel to ensure the structure and content of the microservice don't grow beyond its initially defined scope. As such, the basic components of a microservice are listed here:

- Each microservice should have an API or externally facing mode of communication
- Each microservice, where applicable, should have a unique database component
- Each microservice should only be accessible through its API or externally facing mode of communication

So from what we've learned, microservices vs monolithic architectures could be summed up in the following basic diagram:

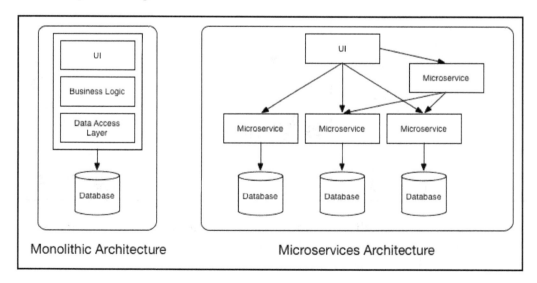

Continuous Integration and Continuous Delivery

Continuous Integration and Continuous Delivery, or CI->CD as they are better known in the software industry, have become a fundamental component of the DevOps movement. The implementation of these practices varies across many organizations. The implementation varies due to a significant variance in CI/CD maturity and evolution.

Continuous Integration represents a foundation for a completely automated build and deployment solution and is usually the starting point in a CI/CD quest. Continuous Integration represents a specific set of development practices, which aim to validate each change to a source-controlled software system through automation. The specific practice of CI in many regards also represents mainline software development coupled with a set of basic verification systems to ensure the commit didn't cause any code compilation issues and does not contain any known landmines.

The general practice of CI is provided here:

1. A developer commits code changes to a source-control system mainline (Per Martin Fowler's invention of CI concepts) performed at least once a day. This is to ensure that code is collaborated on EVEN if they are incomplete.
2. An automation system detects the check-in and validates that the code can be compiled (syntax check).
3. The same automation system executes a set of unit tests against the newly updated code base.
4. The system notifies the committer if there are any identifiable defects related to the check-in.

If at the end of the CI cycle for a given commit there exist any identifiable defects, the committer has two potential options:

1. Fix the issue quickly.
2. Revert the change from the source control (to ensure the system is in a known working state).

While the practice of CI may sound quite easy, in many ways, it's quite difficult for development organizations to implement. This is usually related to the cultural atmosphere of the team and organization.

It is worth noting the source for CI mentioned here comes from Martin Folwer and James Shore. These software visionaries were instrumental in creating and advocating CI implementations and solid development practices. This is also the base platform required for Continuous Delivery, which was created by Jez Humble in 2012.

Continuous Delivery represents a continuation of CI and requires CI as a foundational starting point. Continuous Delivery aims to start by validating each committed change to a software system through the basic CI process described earlier. The main addition that Continuous Delivery offers is that, once the validation of the code change is completed, the CD system will deploy (install) the software onto a mock environment and perform additional testing as a result.

The Continuous Delivery practice aims to provide instant feedback to developers on the quality of their commit and the potential reliability of their code base. The end goal is to keep the software in a releasable form at all times. When implemented correctly, CI/CD provides significant business value to the organization and can help reduce wasted development cycles debugging complex merges and commits that don't actually work or provide business value.

Based on what we described previously, Continuous Delivery has the following basic flow of operations:

- User commits code to source-control mainline
- Automated CI process detects the change
- Automated CI process builds/syntax-checks the code base for compilation issues
- Automated CI process creates a uniquely versioned deployable package
- Automated CI process pushes the package to an artifact repository
- Automated CD process pulls the package onto a given environment
- Automated CD process deploys/installs the package onto the environment
- Automated CD process executes a set of automated tests against the environment
- Automated CD process reports any failures
- Automated CD process deploys the package onto additional environments
- Automated CD process allows additional manual testing and validation

In a Continuous Delivery implementation, not every change automatically goes into production, but instead the principles of Continuous Delivery offer a releasable at anytime software product. The idea is that the software COULD be pushed into production at any moment but isn't necessarily always done so.

Generally, the CI/CD process flow would look like this:

- **Continuous Integration**:

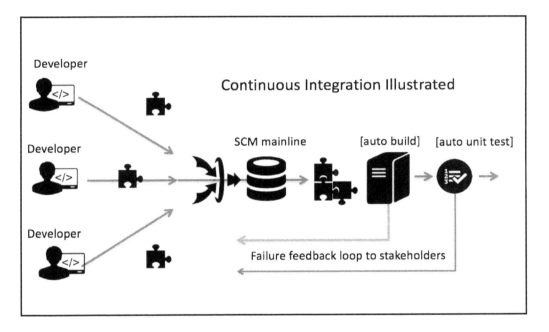

- **Flow of Continuous Delivery**:

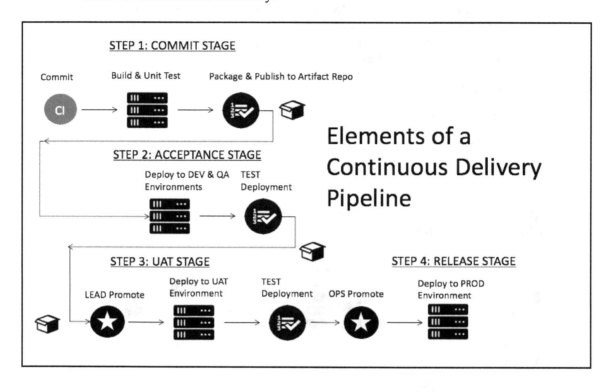

- **Components of Continuous Delivery**:

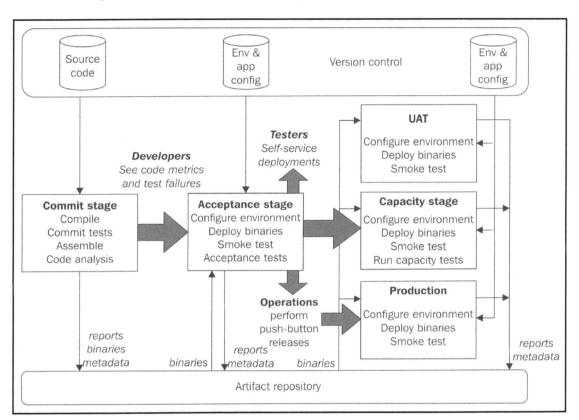

Modularity

Microservices and modularity are similar in nature but not entirely the same. The basic concept of modularity is to avoid creating a monolithic implementation of a software system. A monolithic software system is inadvertently developed in such a way that components are tightly coupled and have heavy reliance on each other, so much so that the effect of updating one component requires the updating of many others just to improve functionality or alleviate the presence of a defect.

Monolithic software development implementations are most common in legacy code bases that were poorly designed or rushed through the development phase. They can often result in brittle software functionality and force the business to continue to spend significant amounts of time updating and maintaining the code base.

On the other hand, a modular software system has a neatly encapsulated set of modules, which can be easily updated and maintained due to the lack of tightly coupled components. Each component in a modular software system provides a generally self-reliant piece of functionality and can be swapped out for a replacement in a much more efficient manner.

Horizontal scalability

Horizontal scaling is an approach to software delivery that allows larger cloud-based organizations to spin up additional instances of a specific services in a given environment. The traffic incoming to this service would then be load-balanced across the instances to provide consistent performance for the end user. Horizontally scaling an application must be approached during the design and development phase of the SDLC and requires a level of discipline on the developer's part.

Blue-green deployments

Blue-green is a development and deployment concept requiring two copies of the product, one called **blue** and other **green**, with one copy being the current release of the product. The other copy is in active development to become the next release as soon as it is deemed fit for production. Another benefit of using this development/deployment model is the ability to roll back to the previous release should the need arise. Blue-green deployments are vital to the concept of CI because, without the future release being developed in conjunction with the current release, hotfixes and fire/damage control become the norm, with innovation and overall focus suffering as a result.

Blue-green deployments specifically allow zero-downtime deployment to take place and for rollbacks to occur seamlessly (since the previous instance was never destroyed). Some very notable organizations have successfully implemented blue-green deployments. These companies include:

- Netflix
- Etsy
- Facebook
- Twitter
- Amazon

As a result of blue-green deployments, there have been some very notable successes within the DevOps world that have minimized the risk of deployment and increased the stability of the software systems.

Artifact management and versioning

Artifact management plays a pivotal role in a DevOps environment. The artifact-management solution provides a single source of truth for all things deployable. In addition to that, it provides a way for the automation system to shrink-wrap a build or potential release candidate and ensure it doesn't get tampered with after the initial build. In many ways, an artifact-management system is to binaries what source control is to source code.

In the software industry, there are many options for artifact management. Some of these are free to use and others require the purchase of a specific tool. Some of the more popular options include:

- **Artifactory** (http://www.jfrog.com)
- **Nexus** (https://www.sonatype.com/)
- **Apache Archiva** (https://archiva.apache.org/index.cgi)
- **NuGet** (https://www.nuget.org/)

Now that we have a basic understanding of artifact management, let's take a look at how an artifact repository fits into the general workflow of a DevOps-oriented environment. A diagram depicting this solution's place within a DevOps-oriented environment is provided next:

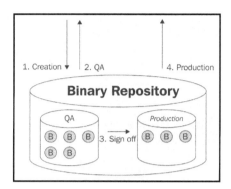

Symmetrical environments

In a rapid-velocity deployment environment (where changes are pushed through a delivery pipeline rapidly), it is absolutely critical that any pre-production and production environments maintain a level of symmetry. That is to say, the deployment procedures and resulting installation of a software system are identical in every way possible among environments. For example, an organization may have the following environments:

- **Development**: Here, developers can test their changes and integration tactics. This environment acts as a playground for all things development oriented and provides developers with an area to validate their code changes and test the resulting impact.

- **Quality-assurance environment**: This environment comes after the development environment and provides QA personnel with a location to test and validate the code and resulting installation. This environment is usually released as a precursor environment, and the environment will need to pass stricter quality standards prior to a sign-off on a given build for release.

- **Stage**: This environment represents the final location prior to production, where all automated deployment techniques are validated and tested.

- **Production**: This environment represents the location where users/customers are actually working with the live install.

Summary

In this chapter, we talked about how DevOps and the DevOps movement began; we learned about the various components of DevOps (CAMS); we discussed the roles agile, Continuous Integration, Continuous Delivery, and microservices have played within DevOps; and we discussed some of the other various architectural techniques that DevOps requires.

In the next chapter, we will delve into configuration management, which also plays a pivotal role in DevOps. By understanding the techniques of configuration management, we will begin to understand the concepts of Infrastructure as Code (which is something Ansible does very well). We will delve into what it means to version your configuration states, how to go about developing code that maintains the infrastructure state, and what the ins and outs are for creating a successful **configuration management (CM)** solution.

2
Configuration Management Essentials

If you are reading this book, you are most likely looking for a consistent way to provision infrastructure, deploy code, and maintain the operational consistency of environments. These items all fit under Configuration Management, or CM for short. Configuration Management represents a cornerstone of DevOps and is something that Ansible manages very well. Configuration Management represents a way of development where automation can be used to provision and enforce the state, consistency, and accuracy of a set of systems. In a DevOps-oriented environment, Configuration Management will become increasingly critical for maintaining development environments, QA apparatuses and systems, production environments, and more. This is because the need to maintain such environments and keep a level of consistency among them is critical for deployment and operational success when it's time to release a software title or update.

In this chapter, we are going to learn all about Configuration Management. The chapter will cover and review how tools such as Ansible can make developers, testers, and operations personnel efforts easier by eliminating environment drift, automating the provisioning of infrastructure, and providing an easy and consistent way to spin up environments that match production. The goal of this chapter is to learn and understand automated Configuration Management techniques, and existentially these Configuration Management techniques could then be applied to provide value to small- or large-scale organizations. Within this chapter we are going to specifically address the following topics:

- Understanding Configuration Management
- Understanding the origins of Configuration Management
- The aims of Configuration Management
- Basic principles of Configuration Management

- Configuration Management best practices
- How Ansible simplifies DevOps implementations
- Binary Artifact Management and Ansible

Configuration Management is such an important topic (especially when it comes to solutions such as Ansible). Shall we get started?

Understanding Configuration Management

Unless you have been living in a bubble, you will probably have seen that Configuration Management automation has taken the IT world by storm. That is to say that hosts can now be automatically configured and provisioned to be in a specific state via code (Packages Installed, Users Created and so on). The idea that infrastructure can be defined and codified is not only novel but is now the norm. Configuration Management in many ways represents to infrastructure what software development represents to end-user software products. If it's unclear at this point what CM actually is, let's quickly define it:

> *Configuration Management is the detailed recording and updating of information that describes an enterprise's hardware and software. Such information typically includes the versions and updates that have been applied to installed software packages and the locations and network addresses of hardware devices.*

Now that we have a basic idea of the textbook definition of CM, let's look at how the definition fits into modern software organizations.

Rapid delivery systems in software have added a significant amount of pressure to maintaining clean and stateful systems in production. This means that the development and rollout schedules of the past are just that: a thing of the past. No longer can companies and their product development teams rest on their proverbial laurels after the launch of a new version of their product. With the rapid adoption of broadband, mobile devices, SaaS, and internet access, consumers now demand more frequent updates at a faster pace than ever before. With such a strong demand and no sign of it easing, automation is a must for any company wishing to manage distribution channels in order to remain competitive in today's fast-paced digital world.

Configuration Management has in many ways changed the landscape of modern development patterns. It has encouraged teams to work more collaboratively, push incremental changes to a software system or IT infrastructure item, manage change-control processes, and track changes as they move from one logical group in an organization to another. While Configuration Management techniques are continuing to evolve (about as fast as technology stacks change), the core concepts of CM are holding steady. These core traits are illustrated in this diagram:

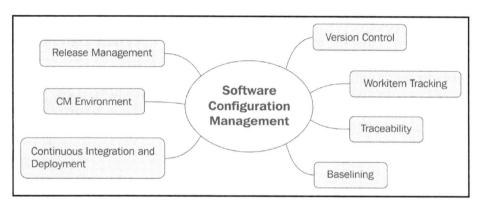

From this diagram, we can see there are a few core tenets of **Software Configuration Management**. These are defined as follows:

- **Release Management**: Release management is the practice of creating automation and processes working in harmony to reliably publish a piece of software for consumption by the target end user.
- **CM Environment**: CM environments represent a set of physical or virtual replications of a production-release environment. As a best practice they should be automatically provisioned through an **Infrastructure as Code** (**IaC**) solution such as Ansible and the infrastructure should be easily replicated using automation.
- **Continuous Integration and Deployment**: Continuous integration and continuous delivery have taken the DevOps world by storm. They are actually an important set of practices that encourage collaboration and span the entire delivery pipeline. These practices are detailed further in later pages.
- **Version Control**: Version control is where all source code and development efforts should be stored. This includes any automated Configuration Management scripts, Ansible playbook's, development code, and automated QA tests.

- **Work item Tracking**: Work item tracking is simply the practice of dividing, tracking, developing, testing and deploying large implementation efforts for a project into smaller, more reasonable chunks that can be worked on individually. Using a work item tracking solution such as JIRA can help small or large teams develop and release solutions more effectively.
- **Traceability**: As a software system, infrastructure-development effort, or quality-assurance automation becomes more complex, it's important to try as far as possible to shrink each work effort into smaller, more easily accomplished tasks. As a result of breaking work items into smaller, more easily accomplished tasks, it's important that the traceability of each change to a given software system be available throughout the delivery pipeline.
- **Baselining**: Baselining an infrastructure solution is important because it provides a solid starting point for *all* future infrastructure implementations. This means that at any given time, you can reimage a system with the known good baseline and build on it from there. In many ways, this also provides a level of consistency.

Origins of Configuration Management

Configuration Management can be traced back in origins to the early 1950s, an era of punch cards and large mainframe computing apparatuses. Punch cards at the time often needed to be organized and delivered to the mainframe, and as a result of this specific ordering, a requirement was mandated by larger organizations to manage the configuration of such punch cards. After the golden days of punch cards, additional management requirements came to light with regard to maintaining the state of a given software system or IT apparatus. Entities capable of managing such a process at the time were limited to the government's **CDC Update** and IBM's **IBM IEBUPDATE**, respectively.

It wasn't until the early to mid 1990s that software Configuration Management (CM for short) began to be taken notice of in mid- to large-scale organizations. Companies and organizations such as IBM and the Department of Defense were among the first adopters of Configuration Management techniques. At this time, Configuration Management was limited in scope to identifying configuration implementations and changes that were added to a given system (or set of systems). This was in an effort to track the steps necessary to recreate the system or deployment if the system were to fail or have some kind of fault. Thus removing the manual efforts that had preceded this innovation.

The Aims of Configuration Management

Configuration Management's goal is to facilitate the lives of developers, quality assurance personnel, management, and operational personnel by providing them with the tools and automation necessary to track and implement additional changes and configurations for a target system. The general logic flow of Configuration Management goes something like this:

> *If I spend four hours configuring a given development system for a developer to use, and then the developer quits the next day, and a new developer gets hired, I have just wasted eight hours. Whereas if I spend eight hours writing a single set of automated scripts to automatically provision a development system and the automation takes 20 minutes to run from start to finish, I can now recreate the developer system easily and with minimal fuss and ceremony.*

On a very basic level, this is what Configuration Management is all about: saving time, saving money, saving resources, and minimizing waste. Yes, it takes a bit of work up front, but the result of such a solution is that machines can be commoditized, black magic won't be required to provision and deploy a given system, and people won't have to work twice as hard to achieve the same goal that a machine can already achieve. In addition to this value point, it also codifies team knowledge, whereas there may be one guy that knows how to setup apache (for example) and if he leaves then management of the solution could continue. As such, the aims of Configuration Management could be defined as follows:

- To track changes made to a given system or set of systems
- To provide traceability and auditability for defects that may arise as part of a set of changes made to a given system
- To help reduce the amount of manual effort made by developers, QA, and operations folks by maintaining a set of automated solutions that can aid in the provisioning and configuration of a given system
- To provide a level of repeatability to the organization by clearly defining (in automation form) the steps required to build out a given system

In the previous simple example, we saw how Configuration Management can save both time and money. But now that we know the basic benefits of Configuration Management and how it's used, let's take a look at a few more examples of CM and how it could potentially benefit an organization.

Scenario 1

Bob works in a large IT software organization as a developer. Bob is working on a bug that he needs some help with. With a proper Configuration Management strategy in place, Bob could easily automate the recreation of his bug environment (the virtual machine used for his local testing and bug recreation efforts) so that both he and his coworker can work on the same bug simultaneously and with minimal fuss in recreating the environment.

In this case, Bob managed to effectively use Configuration Management techniques to not only save his coworker a significant amount of time recreating the bug, but also to remove potential human errors from the equation.

Scenario 2

Taylor is a quality assurance engineer; he has been contacted by Acme Corporation and has been able to successfully recreate a defect on her local machine that is currently plaguing Acme Corporation. Without a proper Configuration Management solution, Taylor would be limited to entering reproduction steps manually into a JIRA ticket and hoping for a speedy remediation of the defect from developers.

Scenario 3

The development team has been working very hard at completing this month's release. The release includes a number of infrastructure changes and environment spin-up requirements. As a result of a solid Configuration Management plan and successful automation, the implementation and rollout of this production release will take a matter of minutes instead of the previous month's hours-long rollout.

Scenario 4

Randy is working hard to help the company's documentation efforts by documenting the recipes of their cloud computing infrastructure. This documentation involves painstakingly recreating the individual components of the system to ensure that new hires have the proper information they need to set up a local working copy of the computing infrastructure. As a result of a solid Configuration Management plan and strategy, Randy has been able to save the numerous hours needed to document this setup solution by simply reading the Configuration Management automation already created and stored in the source control.

As you can see, Configuration Management strategies when used correctly have the ability to save an organization copious amounts of time and, as a result, money in wasted infrastructure costs.

Basic Principles of Configuration Management

Configuration Management aims to help engineering organizations manage the infrastructure, create reusable automation, and provide a strategy for managing change within. As such, Configuration Management purports to provide the following basic principles:

- Automate where automation is possible
- Provide traceability within the enterprise
- Provide developers, QA, operations, and management with a reproducible infrastructure that is managed through software-development best practices
- Develop a strategy for how new hardware will be provisioned and configured (in an automated way)
- Manage hardware configurations effectively and with strategy
- Develop mechanisms that provide a self-service model for deploying infrastructure changes
- Educate the organization on Configuration Management practices

Now that we have a basic understanding of the principles of Configuration Management, let's quickly delve into each of these principles and define them in a bit more depth:

- **Automate everything where automation is possible**: This founding principle of Configuration Management provides us with the guideline that, if a computer can do automatically what a human would do manually, it should be made to do so. While the effort of implementing automation of this type would take time and obviously cost man-hours, the time saved by automating repeatable tasks is significant and the investment upfront would be worth it.

- **Provide traceability in the enterprise**: Most veteran developers have spent time attempting to hunt down a ghost in the machine, whether it's on their local environment or in production. It's equally as frustrating to spend hours trying to determine what specifically changed. The traceability aspect of this concept is important as it provides those who are tasked with determining the fault access to a list of what line of code changed in a given deployment. With a good Configuration Management plan and automation in place, the traceability you seek can be yours.
- **Reproducible infrastructure**: If you have ever spent time at work trying to recreate the build environment for a given software system or reproducing a deployment environment, you know how important this one is. If you have not spent time doing this in the past, you are a lucky person indeed. Oftentimes, one of the biggest time sinks is trying to recreate a development or delivery environment and get all the proper libraries, packages, or modules configured exactly right so the system functions as expected. With a proper Configuration Management solution in place (like Ansible), this is totally possible.
- **Develop a strategy for how new hardware and infrastructure will be automatically provisioned**: This one is probably one of the initial tasks that will need to be done as part of a detailed and comprehensive Configuration Management implementation. With a good plan, the rest will follow.
- **Develop mechanisms for self-service execution of Configuration Management solutions**: In the long run, you don't want to be the gatekeeper of a Configuration Management solution. You will want to plan and create some kind of self-service Configuration Management solution where your customers (developers, QA, operations, and management) can use your solutions via a button click. Some organizations will leverage Jenkins or Circle CI for such tasks. In the end, the solution to use or create is up to you.

Configuration Management Best Practices

Now that we have a basic understanding of Configuration Management's overarching purpose and how it can be leveraged in an enterprise, let's take a look at some best practices involved in Configuration Management. Configuration Management in the modern software enterprise comes in many forms. Some of the more popular tools for Configuration Management are listed as follows:

- Ansible
- Chef

- Puppet
- CFEngine

Solutions such as these are mostly open source options that provide ways to keep and maintain infrastructure in code form, or IaC (Infrastructure as Code). For those unfamiliar with IaC, here is a general definition from Wikipedia:

> *Infrastructure as Code is the process of managing and provisioning computing infrastructure (processes, bare-metal servers, virtual servers, and so on) and their configuration through machine-processable definition files, rather than physical hardware configuration or the use of interactive configuration tools.*

So, from this definition, we can begin to see that **Infrastructure as Code (IaC)** plays an important role in Configuration Management. This is one of the key highlights of Ansible and begins to showcase where it fits into the organization. As such, maintaining infrastructure as code is a Configuration Management best practice.

Another key best practice of a sound Configuration Management strategy is change control. This concept really became popular in the early to mid 1990s and provided development resources with the ability to track changes to source code related to product development. As source control management became more and more popular, people began finding new uses for this solution. Eventually, IaC was stored in source control and this became more essential to effectively managing Configuration Management assets.

As a result of IaC, some organizations began simply tying the **source control management (SCM)** solution into their deployments. This unfortunately violates a best practice of CI/CD that effectively requires artifacts (including automation) to be versioned appropriately and frozen easily so as to allow easy rollbacks and roll-forwards.

Source control systems have come a long way since their early infusion into the software development industry. Modern implementations such as Git and Mercurial have provided new and creative ways of branching, storing source code, and providing offline access to source-code resources. As Configuration Management specialists, it is our job to encourage good practices within source code and help ensure our infrastructure and automation remains of high integrity.

How Ansible Simplifies DevOps Implementations

Ansible is a relatively new player in the software Configuration Management space. Its initial entry into the space was as an open source software creation managed by the team at Ansible in 2012. The name Ansible is derived from the 1980s novel Ender's Game and was selected by Ansible creator, Michael DeHaan. The main effort behind the solution was to provide a simple-to-use and human-readable implementation of a Configuration Management solution.

The initial implementation of Ansible was derived in 2012 and aimed to fit the following principles:

- **Minimal development required**: Configuration Management systems should be lightweight and simplistic in nature.
- **Consistent in execution**: Ansible aims to provide a consistent set of rules and expectations in its core implementation.
- **Secure**: The Ansible platform was developed using SSH as its recommended protocol, which provides a secure transport method for remote execution of Configuration Management code.
- **Scalable**: Whether it's targeting one server or 1,000, the system needs to be able to scale effectively. Ansible has been built with this in mind.
- **Highly reliable in nature**: Providing a consistent execution model is the aim of Ansible—a very reliable execution platform with minimal bugs.
- **Easy to learn**: Eschewing on the complexity of CFEngine and others, Ansible aims to be the easiest-to-learn Configuration Management tool in the industry.

Now that we know the principles Ansible was built upon, let's take a look at how it enhances a DevOps implementation specifically.

Ansible (as we mentioned earlier) was designed to be consistent, easy to manage, scalable, secure, and minimal. With these principles in mind, let's take a quick look at a simple DevOps environment diagram and see how Ansible fits in:

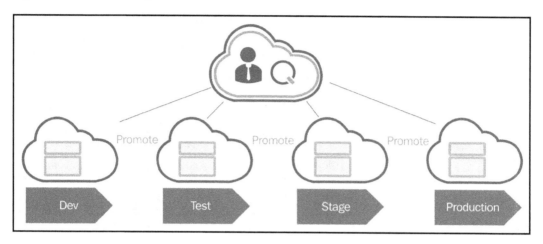

In the diagram, we can see four unique environments (**Dev**, **Test**, **Stage**, and **Production**). These environments are fairly common across DevOps implementations and cloud computing software organizations. Some organizations may have more, some fewer. In a DevOps environment, there may be one or multiple servers or devices that need to be consistently provisioned and deployed to. The consistency across these environments is critical for the eventual release of a software system to production.

Ansible in many ways helps maintain consistency across environments as it provides an easy-to-use automation solution that can be executed in the following manner:

- Simultaneously across environments
- Consistently across environments
- In an idempotent manner that provides a level of congruency across environments

Given the diagram, we can see that each environment would be pushed to symmetrically use a Configuration Management tool such as Ansible. This tool would sit on a central location with access to each of the aforementioned environments. As such, it would be in many ways the governor of the systems. The diagram provided next shows the basic architecture of the push-model architecture that Ansible provides:

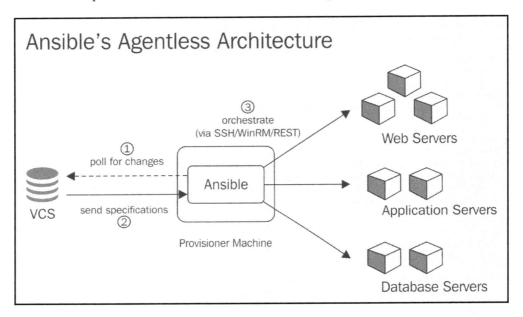

From this diagram, we can see a few things that fit into our Configuration Management best practices list we talked about earlier:

- The Configuration Management resources are stored in a VCS (version control system).
- The Ansible provisioning machine has access to both the VCS and the deployment servers. In some cases, this is good, but in some cases it may be useful to bundle your Ansible resources in with your artifacts (we will talk more about that later).
- Ansible has the ability to target specific server types and configure and deploy to each in a unique way. No matter whether it is the company's web, application, or main database server, Ansible automates otherwise tedious configurations so that we can concentrate on more valuable tasks. This process is done through the development of *playbooks*, or prewritten configuration setups, which save both time and money, as will be discussed later.

Binary Artifact Management and Ansible

In a development project of any scale, anywhere from tens to thousands of artifacts are used, produced, and filed. Most of these digital fragments are in-house resources, but most organizations also utilize libraries and other resources licensed from outside companies, licensed for particular uses and, usually, for contract-specified lengths of time. Managing and complying with these requirements by hand, while possible, would take up far more time than the vast majority of organizations are willing to commit. As such, an artifact-management system should exist to manage these limitations and ensure the same version of any given resource is available to each developer, no matter where they might be. With this in mind, the concept of the artifact repository was born. A central location for all things to be used, created, and managed during the development process resides here until called upon for use in any given software project, however great or small in nature.

Managing dependencies is another important aspect of resource management that cannot be downplayed, as very few software development projects are without dependencies of some sort. Without a system to manage versions and dependencies, our developer Bob from the first *Aims of Configuration Management* scenario might not be able to adequately address a bug that comes up in a ticket. This is due to his lack knowledge of the correct versions of one or more resources that, when combined, cause an issue with how the software functions. These compatibility collisions are common amongst teams who dont maintain a repository for versioned dependencies.

Finally, there is the subject of governance as an important factor in the necessity for a capable binary asset management solution. Since the resources developers use for building software are not only subject to licensing restrictions, and the versions of the resources used are potentially different for each minor/major version of the products being developed, governance is key. Governance requires making sure every resource that sits in our artifact repository has been properly categorized, vetted for quality, and annotated. It ensures that all pertinent licensing and usage requirements have been met and ensures that overall development process flows as smoothly as possible. In addition, governance provides the company with a level of surety that it does not get hit with post-production license issue.

The following is a diagram demonstrating the overall workflow of workstations pulling resources from artifact repository server/machines to use in software development. Once ready to be pushed to production, the completed work is then sent up to the provisioning machine to be paired up with the appropriate playbook. Once paired with the playbook of choice, the change is then sent to the appropriate location for implementation:

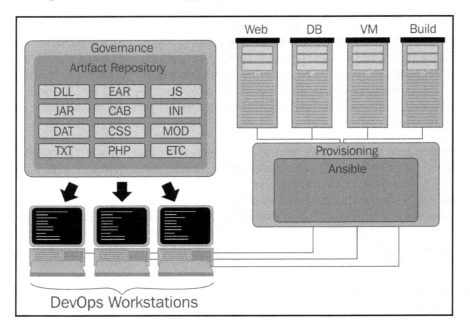

Ansible, a very capable configuration-deployment tool in its own right, is limited in its built-in artifact-management capabilities. Even though many would like Ansible to be a one-stop solution for Configuration Management and deployment, it is but one of many tools in any DevOps team's toolkit to ensure timely deployment of product releases and overall mission success.

Fortunately, all is not lost, as several popular BRM tools are widely used in today's development environments that interface, augment, and complement the capabilities of Ansible while picking up where it leaves off. The following is a list of popular tools that perform well for their respective functions and interface well with Ansible. While popular, the list is neither all-inclusive nor complete, as the market for solutions to this function is always changing, new options being added constantly.

- JFrog's Artifactory (`https://www.jfrog.com/artifactory/`)
- SonaType's Nexus (`https://www.sonatype.com/nexus-repository-sonatype`)
- Apache's Archiva (`https://archiva.apache.org/`)
- Inedo's ProGet (`https://inedo.com/proget`)

With applications such as Archiva and other Maven-based artifact repository managers, Ansible already has packages built in or easily obtainable, such as `maven_artifact` that attempt to grab the required dependencies/artifacts from Maven-based BRMs. For others, such as Nexus, third-party modules exist that serve to make grabbing artifacts from those systems just as easy and painless.

Summary

So far, we have taken a brief ride into what the world of DevOps entails, where it came from, the core principles that make it revolutionary, and its grand rethinking of the processes behind the planning, development, testing, and release of stable software in today's fast-paced world. We also briefly touched on what role Ansible plays in the grand scheme of it all and what makes it so capable of being an important, if not vital, tool in the modern developer's toolkit.

Next, we get into the meat and potatoes of what this book is truly about, which is the software itself. We will learn about it all, from the initial installation of the software on the platform of your choice to ensuring that Ansible is configured properly to talk and interact with various parts of the installed environment so that it can successfully perform its tasks, using the command line of Ansible to navigate the overall setup; and even exploring what core modules are installed as standard, what they do, and where to find more when the need arises.

3
Installing, Configuring, and Running Ansible

Ansible is a relatively new addition to the DevOps and Configuration Management ecosystem. Its radical simplicity, structured automation format, and no brainer development paradigm has caught the eyes of both corporations and startups alike. Organizations such as Twitter have managed to successfully leverage Ansible for highly scaled deployments and Configuration Management implementations across, and have scaled it to manage and deploy to thousands of servers simultaneously. Twitter isn't the only player within the Ansible space that has managed to leverage Ansible at scale; other well-known organizations that have successfully leveraged Ansible include Logitech, NASA, NEC, Microsoft, and hundreds more.

As it stands today, Ansible is in use by some of the largest and well known technology companies and organizations around the world, and is responsible for managing thousands of deployments and maintaining the Configuration Management solutions for countless organizations. Learning the fundamentals of the Ansible solution will provide us with the tools we will need to properly install, configure and run Ansible at small and large scales.

In this chapter, we will formally introduce you to Ansible. Together we will learn how to install it, dive into its run-time architectures, and learn how to configure it to run simple automation sequences. In addition to these topics, we will cover the basics of the Ansible control server under Ubuntu Linux and learn how Ansible can be leveraged for local executions as well as remote management. Finally in this chapter, we will cover the basic concept of a playbook and discover the underlying constructs behind what makes Ansible so powerful. The goals for this chapter will be to grasp the following:

- Installing Ansible
- The Ansible Architecture

- The Ansible Command Line Interface
- Configuring Ansible
- The Ansible Inventory

Now that we have the introductions out of the way let's get started!

Installing Ansible

Ansible itself is cross-platform. The basic installation of the Ansible system is actually fairly easy. Before we can install it, we need to get the Ansible runtime packages. Ansible is available for consumption via the following online solutions:

- Yum (Red Hat Linux-based distributions)
- Apt (Debian)
- Apt (Ubuntu)
- Portage (Gentoo)
- Pkg (FreeBSD)
- macOS (dmg)
- OpenCSW (Solaris)
- Pacman (Arch Linux)
- Pip (Python)
- Tarball (Source)
- Source (Source)

The following is a set of examples and command-line syntaxes for each of the listed options. These commands will help you get up-and-running with Ansible quickly (they are taken from the Ansible website).

Red Hat Enterprise Linux via Configuration Management

Installing Ansible on most popular Red Hat Enterprise Linux flavor distributions is quite easy. This can be accomplished as follows:

```
# NOTE: Before installing Ansible you may need to install the epel-release
repo
# for RHEL or
```

```
# Scientific Linux. Additional details on how to install EPEL can be found
at
# http://fedoraproject.org/wiki/EPEL
$ sudo yum install ansible
```

Apt for Debian/Apt for Ubuntu

Installing Ansible on Debian or Ubuntu flavor Linux distributions is a breeze. This can be accomplished using the Apt package management solution as shown in the following commands:

```
$ sudo apt-get install software-properties-common
$ sudo apt-add-repository ppa:ansible/ansible
$ sudo apt-get update
$ sudo apt-get install ansible
```

Porting Ansible to Gentoo

For Gentoo Linux users, installing Ansible can be accomplished fairly easily. The following command-line syntax can be leveraged to accomplish the installation:

```
# The first command is optional, you may need to unmask the Ansible package
prior to running emerge:
$ echo 'app-admin/ansible' >> /etc/portage/package.accept_keywords
$ emerge -av app-admin/ansible
```

PKG for FreeBSD

FreeBSD-specific users can use `pkg install` to install the Ansible control server solution and get Ansible up-and-running quickly:

```
$ sudo pkg install ansible
```

Pip for macOS

The preferred way to install Ansible for macOS is to use Python's pip installation solution. An example of how to do this is provided next.

If needed, you can install `pip` via the following command:

```
$ sudo easy_install pip
```

Once `pip` is installed, you can install Ansible with the following command:

```
$ sudo pip install ansible
```

OpenCSW for Solaris/SunOS

Solaris users have the ability to install and configure Ansible using the OpenCSW package management solution. This solution can be leveraged as follows:

```
# pkgadd -d http://get.opencsw.org/now
# /opt/csw/bin/pkgutil -i ansiblePacman for Arch Linux
```

Installing Ansible for Arch Linux is quite simple. The following command should help accomplish this task:

```
# Note: If you have Python3 selected you must set
# ansible_python_interpreter = /usr/bin/python2 # in your inventory
variables
$> pacman -S ansible
```

Via Python pip

Prior to installing Ansible using pip we may need to actually install pip. To accomplish this on the command line, the following command can be used:

```
$ sudo easy_install pip
```

Then install Ansible with the following command:

```
$ sudo pip install ansible
```

Once Ansible has been installed

Once Ansible is installed on the desired Linux machine, we will want to verify that it is properly installed and functioning. To do this from the command line, enter the following command:

```
# Display Ansible command line options available
$ ansible --help
# Show the Ansible version number
$ ansible --version
```

Upon successful execution of these commands, Ansible should output version information and related help information respectively.

Setting up authentication between the control server and hosts

When connecting Ansible with remote hosts, Ansible's best practices encourage the use of SSH key sharing. SSH keys allow one Linux host to talk to another without asking for a specific password. In this section we are going to briefly look at how to set SSH key sharing up on the control server and *n* number of target machines.

If SSH key Sharing is not available Ansible also offers the option to ask for a password using the `--ask-become-pass` command-line argument.

To get started, create a `/etc/ansible/hosts` (if it doesn't exist) and add one or more remote systems into its contents. Your specific public SSH key should be located in `authorized_keys` on those target systems.

In this brief tutorial we will assume the SSH key authentication solution is being used. It helps us avoid having to enter or store raw passwords:

```
$ ssh-agent bash
$ ssh-add ~/.ssh/id_rsa
```

Now ping all the nodes (assumes you have an inventory file created):

```
$ ansible all -m ping
```

For a complete documentation set around setting up SSH key sharing in Ubuntu the documentation can be found at `http://linuxproblem.org/art_9.html`.

The Ansible Architecture

Ansible was created with an incredibly flexible and scalable automation engine. It allows users to leverage it in many diverse ways and can be adapted to be used in the way that best suits your specific needs. Since Ansible is agentless (meaning there is no permanently running daemon on the systems it manages or executes from), it can be used locally to control a single system (without any network connectivity) or leveraged to orchestrate and execute automation against many systems, via a control server.

In addition to the aforementioned architectures, Ansible can also be leveraged via Vagrant or Docker to provision infrastructure automatically. This type of solution basically allows Ansible users to bootstrap their hardware or infrastructure provisioning by running one or more Ansible playbooks.

 If you happen to be a Vagrant user, there are instructions within the HashiCorp Ansible provisioning located at the following URL: `https://www.vagrantup.com/docs/provisioning/ansible.html`.

As we mentioned briefly, Ansible is open source, module-based, pluggable, and agentless. These key differentiators from other Configuration Management solutions give Ansible a significant edge. Let's take a look at each of these differentiators in detail and see what it actually means for Ansible developers and users.

Open source

It is no secret that successful open source solutions are usually extraordinarily feature-rich. This is because, instead of a simple eight-person (or even 100-person) engineering team, there are potentially thousands of developers. Each development and enhancement has been designed to fit a unique need. As a result, the end deliverable product provides consumers of Ansible with a very well-rounded solution that can be adapted or leveraged in numerous ways.

Module-based

Ansible has been developed for integration with numerous other open and closed source software solutions. This idea means that Ansible is currently compatible with multiple flavors of Linux, Windows, and cloud providers. Aside from its OS-level support, Ansible currently integrates with hundreds of other software solutions: EC2, JIRA, Jenkins, Bamboo, Microsoft Azure, DigitalOcean, Docker, Google, and many more.

 For a complete list of Ansible modules, consult the official Ansible module support list located at the following URL: `http://docs.ansible.com/ans ible/modules_by_category.html`.

Agentless

One of the key differentiators that gives Ansible an edge against the competition is the fact that it is completely agentless. This means there are no daemons that need to be installed on remote machines, no firewall ports that need to be opened (besides traditional SSH), no monitoring that needs to be performed on remote machines, and no management that needs to be performed on the infrastructure fleet. In effect, this makes Ansible very self-sufficient.

Since Ansible can be implemented in a few different ways, the aim of this section is to highlight these options and help get us familiar with the architecture types that Ansible supports. Generally, the architecture of Ansible can be categorized into three distinct architecture types. These are described next.

Pluggable

While Ansible comes out-of-the-box with a wide spectrum of software integration support, it is oftentimes a requirement to integrate the solution with a company-based internal software solution or a software solution that has not already been integrated into Ansible's robust playbook suite. The answer to such a requirement would be to create a plugin-based solution for Ansible, thus providing the custom functionality necessary.

Local automation execution using Ansible

The easiest way to leverage Ansible is to instruct it to manage a local system. This means there is no need for SSH connections or port openings or SSH key sharing to be done. This implementation simply involves one user, a set of playbooks (or one), and a local system. Local automation execution is the scenario in which Ansible is leveraged to execute a playbook (a series of automation tasks) against a local machine. This specific architecture type means that Ansible does not need an available network connection or internet connection for it to perform its work.

This architecture type is diagrammed next:

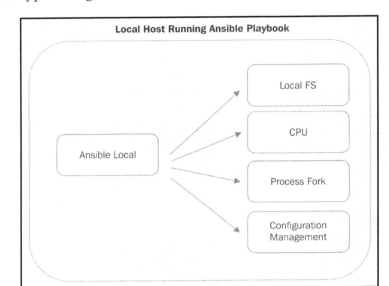

As we can see from the diagram, Ansible can be used for local provisioning. This architecture may seem a bit unscalable, but with a bit of creativity, there is a significant amount of power behind this specific architecture. Let's take a look at some of the various ways in which this specific architecture can be applied:

- To locally provision a development environment and configure it to be a single click setup: ideally with this approach, Ansible playbooks will be written and stored in the local development source control system and then leveraged by new developers to setup and configure their development environments. This will save a significant amount of time on-boarding and getting an employee started.
- To enforce local infrastructure-provisioning rules and revert changes made to the system that were done out of band: this solution would be ideal for enforcing infrastructure that gets tampered with or altered accidentally.
- To execute a set of timed automations that could be leveraged to perform automated routines.

As we can see from the architecture, Ansible's local execution gives us the ability to execute a playbook against a localized system without any fuss or complexity. Let's take a quick look at how to run an Ansible playbook against a local system using the command line. To begin though, let's learn how to run an ad hoc command against a local system. The example is provided as follows:

```
Example: Ad hoc Linux echo command against a local system
#> ansible all -i "localhost," -c local -m shell -a 'echo hello DevOps
World'
```

The command simply tells Ansible to target all systems in the ad hoc inventory implementation (which in our simple use case is only localhost), then execute the command echo "hello DevOps world" against this system. Simple, right? Now let's take a look at how this same implementation might look if it were in Ansible playbook form. An example of this in playbook form is provided as follows:

```
# File name: hellodevopsworld.yml
---
- hosts: all
  tasks:
  - shell: echo "hello DevOps world"
```

This example represents a very simple Ansible playbook. Ansible playbooks are written in **Yet Another Markup Language** (**YAML**). They are intended to be easy to read, easy to write, highly structured, and without complexity. The idea of a *playbook* in the Ansible world comes from the playbook one might receive when attending a broadway show. Playbooks describe in brief the upcoming scenes and actors. As such, Ansible playbooks also contain a list of upcoming events (defined as tasks, and the details of those events). In our simple example, we are telling Ansible to instruct the Linux shell (on the target system(s)) to display a simple introductory message: hello DevOps world.

At this point, you may be wondering, *how does one run such a playbook?* I'm glad you asked. Playbooks can be run from the command line by specifying the playbook name. An example of this is provided here:

```
# Running a Playbook from the command line:
#> ansible-playbook -i 'localhost,' -c local hellodevopsworld.yml
```

Next let's take a look at remote automation execution. This methodology is significantly different from local execution as it allows for much larger scalability support.

Remote automation execution using Ansible

The most popular use of Ansible is through remote execution. This architecture requires a network connection and SSH or Windows remoting. By using remote execution, we are essentially instructing Ansible to reach out over SSH to one or many machines, authenticate using a previously shared SSH or RM key, create a temporary TCP connection to one or more remote machines, and execute a set of playbook-based automations against them. If this sounds a bit confusing, let's take a look in depth at how this architecture and automation solution works.

To begin with, as a local administrator, we will need to pre-authorize the preferred Ansible user with the target machines. By doing this pre-authentication, we are essentially (most commonly through SSH key sharing) configuring at least two Linux-oriented machines (the control and the target) with the permissions needed for the control server to communicate with and control the target machine without further authorization. Details on how to perform a basic SSH key-sharing implementation are covered later in this chapter (or can be found at `http://docs.ansible.com/ansible/intro_getting_started.html`).

Once key sharing has been implemented and has been verified as working, Ansible can effectively take control of the remote systems and execute automation against them. This is accomplished through a nifty self-installation solution provided by Ansible. Effectively, the Ansible automation system (upon execution) will copy itself over to the remote system, install itself on the remote system, run a specified set of playbooks on the target system, verify the results of the execution, and delete itself (and the playbook) from the target system. This leaves the system in the desired state without the need to maintain a running daemon on the target system.

The remote automation execution architecture can be seen via the following illustration:

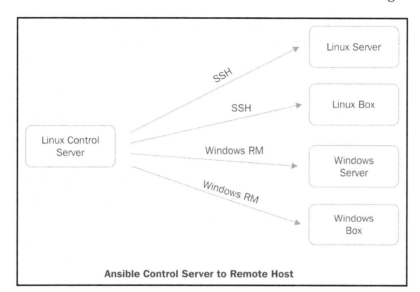

As we can see from the previous diagram, the Linux control server (running Ansible) uses a set of secure protocols (**SSH** and **Windows RM** respectively) to control, automate, and configure the remote systems. These automation executions happen in parallel, meaning that Ansible has the ability to simultaneously control between 1 and 10,000 machines without a significant degradation in performance.

Now that we have a good idea of how a remote execution architecture works, let's take a look at a couple of examples. Ansible (as we discovered in the previous section) leverages playbooks to manage human-readable automation. In this first example, we will need two machines, both Linux based, with Ansible installed on the control server (see the previous diagram for which machine is the control server), and a target server with SSH keys shared so that the control server can properly control or manage the target.

Now to create a playbook, simply edit a file title `hellodevopsworld.yml` and paste the following lines of code into it:

```
# File name: HelloDevOpsWorld.yml
---
- hosts: all
  tasks:
    - shell: echo "hello DevOps world"
```

Save the file onto disk, in a location you prefer (we chose /opt/hellodevopsworld.yml). Next we will need to identify the IP address or HOSTNAME/FQDN of the target machine and run the playbook. For this example our target host is on 192.168.10.10. Now let's run the playbook against the target machine from the control server:

```
# Example command: Execute the playbook hellodevopsworld.yml against
# 192.168.10.10
#> ansible-playbook -i "192.168.10.10," -c local hellodevopsworld.yml
```

From this command, we should see Ansible execute the hellowdevopsworld playbook against the target machine (192.168.10.10) and the execution should output hellodevopsworld to the command-line interface. The following is the output we should see from the executions provided through Ansible:

```
PLAY [all] *********
GATHERING FACTS *********
ok: [192.168.10.10]
TASK: [shell echo "hello world"] *********
changed: [192.168.10.10]
PLAY RECAP *********
192.168.10.10 : ok=2 changed=1 unreachable=0 failed=0
```

By default Ansible is configured to to execute *all* automations in parallel. This can be altered by specifying the --limit option on the command line, which allows the administrator to limit the number of parallel executions to a specific number. This can be handy when you need to be able to debug a playbook or restrict the number of simultaneous executions.

Container-oriented automation

Container-oriented automation is similar to local automation execution, although it leverages the Configuration Management and automation execution capabilities of Ansible on the container. This architecture is slightly different from the others in the sense that it does not rely on Ansible being installed on a given host or container prior to the execution of a playbook but rather installs Ansible on-the-fly (during the provisioning phase of the container) and then executes a playbook once Ansible is installed. As a result, the flow of automation would be better represented through a flow diagram:

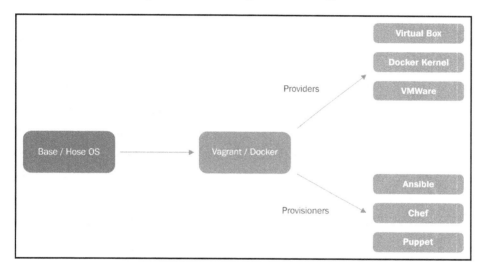

Container-oriented automation can be especially useful for provisioning environments (development, testing, production, and so on) as well as helping get developers up and running quickly. Let's take a look at a quick Vagrant setup using Ansible as the bootstrapping solution within the VM.

To begin, let's log in to our local machine as the `root` user and create a directory setup to hold our local infrastructure. In this example, we are using a macOS machine with VirtualBox and Vagrant (`https://www.vagrantup.com/about.html`) installed (and while these instructions are macOS-specific, they can be applied to Windows machines quite easily as well):

1. Create a directory, which will house our project, and change into it:

```
#> mkdir -p ~/Desktop/helloVagrantAnsible
#> cd ~/Desktop/helloVagrantAnsible
```

2. Initialize Vagrant using the `vagrant init` command:

`#> vagrant init ubuntu/trusty64`

3. Edit the newly created `Vagrantfile`, which should be now located at `~/Desktop/helloVagrantAnsible/Vagrantfile`, to reflect what is shown here (taken from the Ansible website):

```
# This guide is optimized for Vagrant 1.7 and above.
# Although versions 1.6.x should behave very similarly, it is recommended
# to upgrade instead of disabling the requirement below.
Vagrant.require_version ">= 1.7.0"

Vagrant.configure(2) do |config|

 config.vm.box = "ubuntu/trusty64"

 # Disable the new default behavior introduced in Vagrant 1.7, to
 # ensure that all Vagrant machines will use the same SSH key pair.
 # See https://github.com/mitchellh/vagrant/issues/5005
 config.ssh.insert_key = false

 config.vm.provision "ansible" do |ansible|
 ansible.verbose = "v"
 ansible.playbook = "playbook.yml"
 end
end
```

As we can see from the `Vagrantfile`, we are essentially configuring Vagrant to fire up and execute `playbook.yml` upon the initial fire-up. This implementation once understood is incredibly powerful as it provides us with a way of bootstrapping an infrastructure solution with Ansible as its provisioner. This implementation is ideal for developers or quality assurance engineers as it provides them with a way of storing their infrastructure as code.

Now that we have our `Vagrantfile`, let's create `playbook.yml` in the same directory as the `Vagrantfile`. Its contents should reflect the following:

```
# playbook.yml
---
- hosts: all
 tasks:
 - name: "Install Apache"
 apt: name={{ item }} state=present
 with_items:
 - apache2
```

```
- name: "Turn on Apache and set it to run on boot"
  service: name={{ item }} state=started enabled=yes
  with_items:
  - apache2
```

This playbook (as you may have guessed) simply installs Apache2 on the Ubuntu system we defined in our `vagrant init` command and tells Ansible to provision it with Apache enabled as a system service at boot.

The final step in this tutorial is to simply run our Vagrant setup by typing the following command into our command-line window:

```
# Start Vagrant and auto provision the system with Ubuntu,
# Ansible and Apache
$> vagrant up
```

If everything was successful, you should be able to see your local Apache instance running within the VirtualBox provisioned and running through Vagrant.

The Ansible Command-Line Interface

Ansible provides a robust command-line interface, which provides users with the ability to run Ansible playbooks, simulate the execution of Ansible playbooks, run ad hoc commands, and much more. In the Ansible galaxy (more to come on that specific pun later in the book), there are two specific types of Ansible commands that can be run. The `ansible` command allows users to run ad hoc commands, whereas the `ansible-playbook` command allows the user to execute a set of Ansible playbook instructions against the targeted infrastructure.

This is ambiguous within the documentation, Ansible and Ansible-playbook appear to be symlinks but there are some reports of different functionality between the two. More research is needed before final drafting to ensure accuracy of information reported. For now, there will be a section for Ansible and Ansible-playbook (provided in the following sections) but these may change going forward.

The Ansible command-line interface is the gateway into the heart of Ansible and provides a wide array of options and configurable switches that will help you gain the most out of Ansible. Let's take a quick tour of the Ansible command-line interface and see what the available switches and knobs do.

Usage: ansible <host-pattern> [options]

In this section we are going to take a look at the Ansible command-line patterns and see how they function. The implementation of the command line solution for Ansible is actually quite easy to understand. Let's take a look at a couple of easy examples.

The `--help` option will display a complete list of available command-line options. This is probably one of the most important command-line options within the Ansible CLI:

Help: [#> ansible --help]

Now that we know how to use the `help` command let's take a look at the `version` command. This command-line argument provides us with the version information for the Ansible installation we are using:

Version: [#> ansible --version]

The `ansible --version` command will output the version information for the installed copy of Ansible. For example, you might see something like the following:

```
#> ansible --version
ansible 2.0.0.2
config file = /etc/ansible/ansble.cfg
configured module search path = Default w/o overrides
```

Now that we understand the `version` command, let's see how to check our playbook's syntax and perform a test run of our playbook. This is accomplished through the `--check` option:

Check: [#> ansible foo.yml --check]

This command-line option allows you to see what some of the changes Ansible would have made would potentially be. This is a great way to simulate the execution of a playbook and is a wise first step before actually running one:

Inventory: [#> ansible -i 192.x.x.x, x.x.x.x]

Specifying an inventory on the command line is important. It is accomplished via the -inventory-file parameter. This command-line parameter allows us to specify a comma-separated list of hostnames that will be targeted by the execution of the playbook. This command line allows you to specify a path location to an Ansible inventory file (in YAML format). Inside it, you can specify the hostnames and groups that combined make up your infrastructure inventory (the host's Ansible will be targeted during execution):

InventoryFile: [#> ansible -inventory-file 192.x.x.x, x.x.x.x]

This command-line option instructs Ansible to display a list of targeted hosts for this execution. This can be useful when you have a large number of hosts separated into groups and you only want to target a subset of those hosts:

```
ListHosts: [#> ansible -list-hosts]
```

This command-line option instructs Ansible to condense all logging output to one line. This includes the facts-gathering processes, task execution output, and all STDOUT output:

```
OneLine: [#> ansible --one-line]
```

This command-line option instructs Ansible to pipe all output to a specific file instead of the traditional console location. Output in the file specified will be concatenated in the file:

```
Output: [#> ansible --output <filename>]
```

This command-line option instructs Ansible to perform a syntax check on the specified playbook instead of executing it. This is useful for developers who want to ensure their playbook is in valid YAML format prior to execution:

```
SyntaxCheck: [#> ansible --syntax-check]
```

This command-line option instructs Ansible to override the default timeout (in seconds) from 10 to another number:

```
TimeOut: [#> ansible -timeout=X]
```

This command-line option instructs Ansible to use a remote user login instead of the default SSH shared keys approach when connecting to remote hosts. This can be useful if SSH access is not allowed when connecting to some hosts:

```
User: [#> ansible -u | --user =USERNAME]
```

This command-line option instructs Ansible to add verbose logging to the output of the execution. This is handy when debugging specific host issues or odd behavior that isn't expected from traditional execution:

```
Verbose: [#> ansible -verbose]
```

 For additional command-line options, consult the Ansible CLI online help or documentation. Additional online help can be found at http://www.ansible.com.

Ansible command-line examples

Now that we have a pretty good understanding of the various knobs that the Ansible command line provides, let's take a look at a few examples of how to use them to enhance the execution of a playbook. The following examples show some basic ways in which Ansible can be leveraged to run:

```
Example: Run an ad hoc command against an Ansible inventory group and limit
the execution of a playbook to a max of 5 simultaneous servers:
$ ansible europe -a "whoami" -f 5

Example: Execute a playbook against the Europe group as a privileged
account (different from the SSH account
$ ansible europe -a "/usr/bin/foo" -u username --become [--ask-become-pass]

Example: Transfer a local (on the ansible control server) file to a set of
remote hosts simultaneously
$ ansible europe -m copy -a "src=/opt/myfile dest=/opt/myfile"

Example: Running an ansible playbook against a single hostname or IP
address
#> ansible-playbook -i "192.168.10.10," -c local hellodevopsworld.yml

Example: Running an ansible playbook against an inventory group
#> ansible-playbook myplaybook.yml
```

Configuring Ansible

Ansible maintains a central configuration file, which is used to instruct Ansible on how to behave. Ansible's primary configuration file should be located (for most Linux distributions) at the following location:

```
/etc/ansible/ansible.cfg
```

This configuration file instructs Ansible on how to behave at runtime. During the pre-startup sequences of Ansible's execution, the configuration file is loaded into memory and sets a number of environmental flags. These flags and configuration options can help you customize the Ansible runtime. The following configuration is a snapshot of the ansible.cfg file.

Nearly all Ansible configuration options can be overridden via modifications in a playbook. Changes to this configuration file will give you the ability to set base functionality/configuration.

The Ansible configuration file has a pretty detailed set of documentation items associated with each configurable option available. As such, it would be redundant to provide a complete configuration file walk-through within this section. Instead, let's take a look at the more commonly tweaked configuration options.

Common base configuration items

The most common base configuration items are predefined within Ansible; these values however can be overridden through the `ansible.cfg` file and customized to suit your specific needs. To override any one of them, simply uncomment the line (by removing the # symbol in front). These configuration items are provided as follows:

```
# some basic default values...

#inventory = /etc/ansible/hosts
#library = /usr/share/my_modules/
#module_utils = /usr/share/my_module_utils/
#remote_tmp = ~/.ansible/tmp
#local_tmp = ~/.ansible/tmp
#forks = 5
#poll_interval = 15
#sudo_user = root
#ask_sudo_pass = True
#ask_pass = True
#transport = smart
#remote_port = 22
#module_lang = C
#module_set_locale = False
```

In addition to the base configuration overrides, Ansible has a few other interesting configuration tweaks that can be made to the base installation that provide some level of flexibility in its operational functionality.

Disable host key checking (useful for auto provisioning new systems) by using this:

```
#host_key_checking = False
```

By default, the system is configured to run Ansible playbooks as `root`; however, this is not always desirable. To alter this, simply uncomment the following line and specify the user you would like to use instead:

```
# default user to use for playbooks if user is not specified
# (/usr/bin/ansible will use current user as default)
#remote_user = root
```

Sometimes disabling logging is a good thing (for those with limited space options). To disable logging, change the following configuration item:

```
# prevents logging of task data, off by default
#no_log = False
```

The Ansible Inventory

Ansible maintains a central configuration file, which is used to identify and maintain the infrastructure identifications. This inventory file allows the Ansible administrator/ playbook to easily list, group, and target infrastructure items during execution. The default Ansible inventory file created (upon installation of Ansible) is /etc/ansible/hosts. Inside it are a few examples of basic inventory grouping structures and organizational categories for infrastructure.

In general, the Ansible inventory file can be leveraged to organize hosts in a couple of specific ways: as a set of defined groups, or as a set of defined infrastructure pieces (loosely defined and not in a specific group). The inventory file can leverage either of the previously described methods or a combination of the two. Let's look in greater detail on how these two inventory organization systems operate.

Defined inventory groups

Ansible provides a robust and feature-rich mechanism for managing the information related to the infrastructure it controls. Specifically, inventory files can be created to define the infrastructure that will be managed by Ansible. An Ansible inventory file as you may have guessed is also in YAML format. Inventory items (such as servers or devices) are typically defined within the inventory file and are often organized into logically respective groups. An example of these types of groups (with inventory items defined within) is shown within the following code block:

```
[databaseservers]
mydbserver105.example.org
mydbserver205.example.org

[webservers]
mywbserver105.example.org
mywbserver205.example.org
```

Based on this information, we can see there are two groups: a web server and a database server group. These groups each have two unique servers assigned to them and as such provide us with the ability to target either or both groups of infrastructure by group name.

 Ansible inventory items don't have to be unique to one group specifically. Ansible supports the idea that hostnames or IPs can belong to one or many groups. For example, a hostname may exist both in the web server group and the database group. This adds significant flexibility within the Ansible playbook execution system.

Ansible by nature allows this grouping to be targeted asynchronously. This means that the automation can be executed in parallel across either group to target a specific group specified in the hosts inventory file.

Loose inventory items/hosts/devices

Ansible provides the ability to not group any specific hosts that you want. Or mix and match grouped hosts with 'loose hosts'. This functionality allows the Ansible developer or user to simply add raw hostnames into the inventory host file and not attach it to a specific group. For this specific implementation, the hosts file would look something like the following:

```
loosehost.example.com

[webservers]
foo.mycorp.com
bar.mycorp.com

[dbservers]
apple.mycorp.com
pear.mycorp.com
peaches.mycorp.com
```

As you can see from the screenshot, the raw entries that are not grouped are simply organized by IP address or hostname at the top of the inventory hosts file. This allows you to target these hosts by default automatically and without specifying a targeted group name on the command line.

Executing playbook's and targeting specific inventory files and groups

Now that we have a set of inventory groups or raw inventory items defined, the next step is to see how to call Ansible and target a specific set of groups or even inventory files (if different from the default /etc/Ansible/hosts file). This functionality is incredibly important as we gain experience using Ansible. Let's take a look at how to target specific groups first. The following example provides a simple example of an Ansible command line that executes a playbook against a grouped inventory:

```
#> ansible playbookfoo.yml -l 'groupname'
```

As we can see from the example, we can execute Ansible playbooks against specific infrastructure groups. The outcome of these executions is the execution of a set of automated tasks against the group's infrastructure.

Summary

In this chapter, we discussed the various architecture types that Ansible provides, we talked about how inventory files work, and how to target specific groups and servers using the -l command. We also talked about how to install, set up, and configure Ansible to work under most common conditions. In our examples we look at a lot of Ubuntu specific implementations but the conversion to other OS's should be easy.

In the next chapter, we will learn all about playbook files and inventory file extensibility as well as how to create additional inventory files to help manage your infrastructure more effectively. Playbook's represent the heart and soul of the Ansible platform and instruct it on how to behave on a given server or infrastructure.

By the time we complete the next chapter, we should begin to have the skills you will need to write a playbook and execute it against one of a few machines. In addition, you should be able to perform most basic Configuration Management and deployment tasks using Ansible. Also, upon completing this chapter, you should have a solid understanding of how Ansible inventories work and how to effectively create groups and manage infrastructure at scale.

4
Playbooks and Inventory Files

As we discovered in the previous chapters, Ansible offers unique, easy-to-comprehend implementations for creating automation, implementing Configuration Management solutions, maintaining infrastructure, and scaling out automation. Automation and Configuration Management implementations are developed and maintained using Ansible playbooks (as we discussed in the previous chapter), whereas infrastructure inventory is managed through one or many Ansible inventory hosts file. A playbook in Ansible is really quite simple to understand; it's simply a set of tasks to execute that are ordered in a structured format. These two very easy-to-understand concepts have helped pave the way and made Ansible as popular and robust as it is today.

The concept of an Ansible playbook is an easy one to grasp and understand. The same can be said for the the implementation of Ansible inventory files. Playbook's and roles in Ansible make up the bulk of the automation we will be developing throughout this book and are a core construct of the Ansible implementation. This chapter however will focus on Playbook's and Inventory files specifically. Inventory files exist to help us maintain the infrastructure we will target via a playbook and allow us to group similar devices and infrastructure when targeting remote hosts. These two constructs combined provide a highly scalable automation solution that can be used to maintain one machine or 10,000.

In this chapter, we will discuss and learn all about Ansible playbook's and Inventory solutions, and learn how to develop, maintain, and expand an Ansible footprint within an organization. The learning areas we are going to cover will include the following topics:

- Ansible Playbook Constructs
- Ansible Play's and Task's
- Variables and Variable Files
- Hosts and Inventory

- Targeting Infrastructure
- Ansible Modules

As we progress through this chapter, we will try to gain a clear understanding of how Ansible playbooks are created and how to create automation that is fault tolerant, robust, and easy to maintain.

Ansible Playbook Constructs

The Ansible playbook is at the heart of the Ansible Configuration Management and Automation System. Each playbook is made up of one or more plays. The concept of a playbook was derived from sporting references, where a coach would create a set of plays off the field and execute them during a game. The creators of Ansible leveraged this idea to create and successfully deliver an easy-to-use automation and Configuration Management solution. Playbook's are developed using YAML (more about this in the next section), and optionally Jinja2 for more comprehensive automation implementations.

Ansible playbook comprise a few specific structural and formatting elements, namely the following:

- YAML syntax (the language Ansible leverages for automation)
- Jinja2 (optional)
- The hosts section (which defines the host groups to target during execution)
- One or many configuration overrides (this section allows playbook developers to override configuration options or set specific playbook flags)
- The vars section (optional)
- Plays with tasks inside them

 In addition to these elements, YAML (and by nature Ansible) supports commenting within the YAML file. Comments are simply notation documentation that has no programmatic meaning but is useful for developers and playbook authors to keep notes within the playbook directly. Comments in YAML are initiated with the # operator, and everything on that line after the # is ignored by YAML and Ansible.

Let's spend a few minutes looking at the hosts, vars, and play sections of an Ansible playbook and learn how we can leverage them to create effective and maintainable automation.

The programming languages that make up a playbook

In the Ansible world, playbook's are developed using YAML and Jinja. **YAML** stands for **YAML Ain't Another Markup Language**, and Jinja2 is its own independent name. Of the two, YAML is the primary language whereas Jinja is supplementary.

YAML

As mentioned earlier, YAML™ is the primary language used to create playbooks. But what exactly is YAML? Here is what `http://yaml.org/` has to say on the subject:

> *"YAML (rhymes with "camel") is a human-friendly, cross language, Unicode based data serialization language designed around the common native data types of agile programming languages. It is broadly useful for programming needs ranging from configuration files to internet messaging to object persistence to data auditing. Together with the Unicode standard for characters (*`http://unicode.org/`*), this specification provides all the information necessary to understand YAML version 1.2 and to create programs that process YAML information."*

As described in the excerpt, YAML is designed to be human-friendly. This means that while it can contain data and basic logic (typically provided by Jinja2), it emphasizes the concept of readability and convention over complexity and features. Additional information on YAML can be found at `http://www.yaml.org`.

YAML uses tab-indented formatting and key/value pair dictionaries to express the data that is inside a given YAML file. This makes it parseable for Ansible and makes it easy to read at the same time. YAML's unique yet simplistic structure provides Ansible playbook developers with a guess-free way of developing playbooks and ensuring that they will be executable through Ansible. While YAML's structure is easy to read, sometimes it's tabbing can trip some users up. Let's take a look at a couple of simple examples of YAML files and see what the basic data structure looks like:

```
# Simple YAML Data Structure
---
planets:
  - earth: 'welcome to earth'
    species: humans

  - mars: 'we come from mars'
    species: martians
```

From the previous example, we can easily see the content is simply a list of planets, species, and greetings. Are we saying that all YAML really is is an easy-to-read way of managing lists? In a way, yes. Let's explore this idea further.

Basic data in YAML is structured into key/value pairs; the information is organized by indentation. For programmers, this is nothing surprising, but for a novice this may sound confusing. A basic key/value-paired data structure is similar to a list of items. In a key/value data structure, there are two intrinsically linked data items. A **key** is essentially a pointer, which references the value. The **value** can be raw data (a simple bit of text) or even another set of key/value pairs. This makes managing lists of key/value pairs very easy. The indentation in YAML syntax makes organizing the data it represents easy to read. It ensures that nothing is garbled or badly formatted and the information is easily identifiable and legible.

As we can see from the previous YAML example, YAML is a well-formatted (tab-enforced) language. Tabs in YAML are a bit of a misnomer, as you can't actually use the Tab key. Use spaces instead. Tabs are forbidden in YAML because different text editors provide different implementations of tabbing and the implementations are not consistent.

Jinja2 – a brief introduction

Jinja on the other hand is a bit more feature rich than YAML. It has been integrated into Ansible's runtime engine and provides a bit of the more scripting language-like features that developers are used to. Its syntax fits nicely into YAML (as described previously) and allows the developer to use things such as conditionals, loops, variable substitution, and environment variable retrieval. Further information related to jinja2 and its syntax can be found at `http://jinja.pocoo.org/docs/2.9/`. Let's take a quick look at some basic Jinja syntax:

```
# Simple Jinja syntax
{{my_var}}
```

This code doesn't look very useful at first, but once we put it in context, it becomes much more valuable. Let's take a peek at how Jinja fits in with YAML:

```
# Example Jinja Playbook
- hosts: all
  vars:
    foo: "{{ lookup('env', 'FOO' }}"
  tasks:
    - name: Copy file
      copy: src="{{ foo }}" dest=/some/path mode=0775 owner=user group=user
```

This simple example of an Ansible playbook with YAML and Jinja combined provides a way for us to use the contents of a system environment variable within our playbook. We will go into this type of implementation in much more detail later within this book, but for now, we at least can see one structured example of how Jinja can be leveraged within a YAML file.

 Jinja offers many more solutions and manipulations of an Ansible playbook, which we will discuss in Chapter 6, *Jinja in Ansible*. This introduction is simply to provide you with an understanding of how YAML and Jinja can coexist.

Constructing an Ansible playbook

YAML's unique and well-formatted syntax provides a highly structured yet human-readable format for expressing data. More specifically, YAML's data structure is expressed in lists, with each list item containing key/value pairs (or dictionaries). At the beginning of each YAML file, YAML optionally supports a --- initiator (to notate the beginning of the YAML file), and conversely, at the end of each, YAML supports a . . . terminator, which (as you may have guessed) indicates the end of a YAML file. Let's take a look at a very simple playbook as an example:

```
---
- hosts: all
  vars :
    http_port : 80
    tasks:
    - name: Install nginx web server
      apt: pkg=nginx state=installed update_cache=true
      notify:
        - start nginx
```

Now that we have seen an example of an Ansible playbook, let's look at the possible available sections within a playbook, and see what each does.

Hosts

The hosts section is where we can target groups of inventory. The inventory in Ansible represents one or many devices that Ansible can connect to and run automation against.

Variables (vars/vars_files)

The `vars` and `vars_file` sections of an Ansible playbook contain a set of variable data that can be used later in the playbook. This information is known as **facts**. The variable concept in Ansible is identical in nature to computer programming variables but with different scopes, depending on where it's defined.

Tasks/plays

The aim of Ansible plays is to connect one or more groups of hosts to a set of roles, represented by things, which Ansible calls tasks. At its most basic definition, an Ansible task is nothing more than a callout to an Ansible module.

Great; we now have a basic understanding of the sections that make up a playbook, but we really don't know how to effectively use them to create a playbook or how to target a specific set of servers or infrastructure.

Ansible Play's and Task's

As we have already discovered, within the heart of the Ansible configuration and Automation System is the the playbook. The most important element of the playbook is the idea of plays and tasks. Plays represent a categorization of a collection of Ansible tasks, whereas tasks are individual automation steps that make up the play.

Consider plays as the overarching grouping and tasks as the items that reside within a given play. For example, you may have a database play, a web server play, or even a load balancer play. In this section, we will discover how plays and tasks work in the Ansible world.

Ansible plays

Ansible plays are named after sports plays. In YAML, plays are represented via one or more tasks sections within a playbook. The plays section (or sections) of an Ansible playbook represents the heart of the Ansible automation engine. In Ansible, each task has a name (a user-friendly description of the action to be executed) and a set of parameters that define how the system should execute, report on, or handle the aftermath of the execution. Let's take a look at a couple of ways in which we can implement Ansible plays within a given playbook.

The example provided next provides us with a glimpse into an Ansible playbook with a single play:

```
tasks:
    - name: Can we use Ansible to Install Apache2 web server
      apt: pkg=apache2 state=installed update_cache=true
```

Looks pretty basic, right? Plays can have one or more tasks underneath them. They are pretty easy to read and very easy to write. However, a playbook does not need to be isolated into a single play. For example, we could just as easily do something like the following:

```
tasks:
    - name: Use Ansible to Install nginx web server
      apt: pkg=nginx state=installed update_cache=true

tasks:
    - name: Use Ansible to Install MySQL web server
      apt: pkg=mysql-server state=installed update_cache=true
```

This second example is also human-readable but has two specific plays defined within. The first play handles the installation of nginx, whereas the second play handles the installation of the MySQL server. By using multiple plays in a single playbook, we can group automation into a single playbook yet segregate the actual tasks. Neat, huh? Now that we have a good understanding of what an Ansible play is, let's take a look at Ansible tasks.

Ansible tasks

In the previous section, we talked primarily about Ansible plays. Underneath a given play is a set of Ansible tasks. Ansible tasks can perform numerous actions on a local or target system. This includes installing packages (such as `apt`, `yum`, and `opencsw`), copying files, starting services, and much, much more. Ansible tasks make up the glue that binds automation and human-readable actions. Let's take a look at the elements of the Ansible tasks section and see how to write them:

```
tasks:
  - name: <some description>
    <API>: PARAM1=foo PARAM2=foo PARAM3=foo
```

This snippet is pretty simplistic; there is a single play (notated by tasks:) and a single task underneath the play. Within the task itself, the name parameter has (in plain English) a description of what we are trying to accomplish when this task is executed. The <API> tag on the next line (below the `name` definition) will simply be the Ansible module we are invoking. After the module `name`, there is a set of parameters that are passed to the module that specify more granularly the details about the module we are invoking. So to have a better real-world example, let's take a look at the following code excerpt:

```
tasks:
    - name: Can we use Ansible to Install nginx web server
        apt: pkg=nginx state=installed update_cache=true
```

The aforementioned play simply tells Ansible to install the nginx web server on an Ubuntu-based system. We know this because the module the task is calling is `apt` and the parameters instruct Ansible to ensure the package (`pkg`) `nginx` is in the state installed. Additionally, prior to installing the package, we have also instructed the `apt` module to update its local cache. Simple, right?

One of the nicest things about Ansible is its ability to skip over tasks that will not effect change on a given system. For example, if the package `nginx` is already installed, Ansible will skip the step entirely as it is smart enough to know that the `nginx` package already exists on the system.

So now that we know the basic structures of an Ansible playbook, we will want to know how to extend our playbooks to handle more complex parameters within our tasks. The next step in this learning process is understanding multiline parameters. Let's proceed.

Multiline task parameters

Some Ansible tasks can have a bunch of parameters (so much so that the simplicity and readability of the task become ambiguous). The YAML implementation has also matured in such a way as to support parameters across multiple lines for better readability. This is specifically a *scalar folded approach* that is available within the YAML language directly. Let's take a look at an example provided by the YAML creators to understand how line folding works in YAML:

```
# Multiple-line strings can be written either as a 'literal block' (using
|),
# or a 'folded block' (using '>').
literal_block: |
    This entire block of text will be the value of the 'literal_block' key,
    with line breaks being preserved.
```

```
The literal continues until de-dented, and the leading indentation is
stripped.

        Any lines that are 'more-indented' keep the rest of their
indentation -
        these lines will be indented by 4 spaces.
folded_style: >
    This entire block of text will be the value of 'folded_style', but this
    time, all newlines will be replaced with a single space.

    Blank lines, like above, are converted to a newline character.

        'More-indented' lines keep their newlines, too -
        this text will appear over two lines.
```

So in the context of Ansible playbook's we can use the scalar folded approach to perform multiline playbook tasks. As a result, we can reformat a task as follows:

```
# Initial task definition
tasks:
    - name: Can we use Ansible to Install nginx web server
      apt: pkg=nginx state=installed update_cache=true

# Same task using the scalar folded approach to task definitions
tasks:
    - name: Can we use Ansible to Install nginx web server
      apt: >
        pkg=nginx
        state=installed
        update_cache=true
```

Multiline implementations of Ansible tasks are based on preference and formatting. So in some cases you may have a playbook task that is really long and in that case you would want to consider using a multiline task. On the converse, shorter playbook tasks would probably not need such an implementation. Again its simply a matter of readability and preference.

Now that we have a good idea of how to better organize our playbook data structures, let's look at variables and how those fit into our playbook creation process.

Variables and Variable Files

Variables are a critical part of any scripting or development language, and Ansible is no different. Variables act as named placeholders for data elements, important information, numerical values, and more. Ansible provides a `vars` section and a `vars_files` section, which are optionally included in a playbook. Variables defined here are playbook-centric and can be used within the playbook. These sections of the playbook allow us to define variables in two unique ways. Let's look at an example to better understand how variables are defined:

```
---
- hosts: all
  vars:
    myvar: helloworld
  vars_files:
    - /vars/my_vars.yml
```

As we can see from the example, we can be rather creative when defining variables that Ansible can use in its playbook. Variables can be specified via the `vars` section, the `vars_files` section, or even via the command line through the `ExtraVars` parameter. Let's take a look at the key/value implementation of variables as well as a `vars_file` implementation and discover how these can be leveraged to provide reusable data to our Ansible playbooks.

Basic variable syntax

The most obvious solution for managing variables within Ansible is to leverage the key/value vars section in the beginning of an Ansible playbook, which allows us to define a set of simple key/value datasets that we can make available to the remaining tasks in our playbook.

The `vars` section in an Ansible playbook provides us with an easy location from where we can create a list of globally available Ansible variables. Ansible reads this `vars` section and its associated key/value based variables during the initialization of a playbook (specifically, during the facts-gathering phase). Each data item retrieved during this phase is known as a **fact**. The variables can then be used elsewhere in the playbook.

Let's look at a few examples of key/value variable sets in Ansible and how to use them in a playbook:

```
Example: Simple Key/Value Variables in Ansible.
---
- hosts: all
  vars:
    # Single Variable(s) Example
    myvar: helloworld

  tasks:
    - name: $myvar
      ping:
```

The example shows how to create and use a simple $myvar variable and use it in a playbook play. Next, let's look at a slightly different implementation of Ansible variables (at the task level). Consider the following playbook fragment:

```
# Task specific variables
tasks:
  - name: copy files
    copy: src={{ item }} dest=/opt/{{ item }}
    with_items:
      - foo
      - bar
```

In the example, we have illustrated a simple iterative loop of sorts to copy the files foo and bar into the specified destination. Now that we have a good idea of basic Ansible variables, let's take a look at some more scalable ways to manage Ansible variable data.

Variable files

As we just discussed, Ansible has the vars section within a playbook. This is perfectly sufficient for a limited number of data points. However, if the amount of information is expected to grow or pertain to various environments, the vars section can get highly unwieldy if not managed carefully. Instead of using the vars section for managing data, we can use a vars file (or many vars files). A vars file represents a way to encapsulate a set of data points into an external file on the Ansible control server's disk. We then specify the vars file in our Ansible playbook, and Ansible will load it at the appropriate time.

When using a `vars` file, it's important to note that we can include the `vars` file in our playbook in a couple of possible locations: a `vars_file` section or within an Ansible task (task-specific scoped). The examples provided next will help better illustrate this.

Let's look at an example of the `vars` files in action. The following example shows the contents of a simple `vars` file:

```
east_coast_host_local: virginia
west_coast_host_local: oregon
definitions:
- servers: web
    instance: apache
- servers: db
    instance: cassandra
ping_server: 192.168.10.10
```

As we can see from the content of the `vars` file, it's nothing more than a YAML file. Who would have guessed? The neat thing here really isn't its content but rather the construction. But before we move on to any really neat things, let's take a look at how to reference the file and data within via a playbook. The corresponding playbook for the previous `vars` file is as follows:

```
# Example: Simple Variables File in Ansible.
---
- hosts: all
  vars_files:
    - my_vars_file.yml

  tasks:
    - name: ping target server
      ping: $ping_server
```

So based on the content of this playbook, we can see that it simply has an added `vars_file` section, which is loaded during startup.

These two file examples are very simple in nature. Let's look at another way of loading a variables file based on the context of the aforementioned examples. Here is an alternate playbook:

```
# Example: Simple Variables File in Ansible.
---
- hosts: all
  tasks:
    - name: include default step variables
      include_vars: my_vars_file.yml
```

```
    ping: $ping_server
```

So we can see based on this code provided that we can scope a `vars` file to a specific task as well. This can be very handy for altering certain data points in a task based on specific criteria (per environment or per host).

Now that we have a good idea of how `vars` files work, let's take a look at one more example of how a `vars` file might be leveraged:

```
# Example: Simple Variables File in Ansible.
---
- hosts: all
  vars_files:
    - my_vars_file.yml
    - "/opt/varsfiles/{{ env_vars }}.yml"
  tasks:
    - name: ping target server
      ping: $ping_server
```

Can you guess what this will do yet? Let's take a look at how we might execute this playbook from the command line for a hint:

```
$> ansible-playbook site.yml -e "env_vars=dev" -c local
```

Okay so let's understand how this works. Basically, the command specifies a variable of `env_vars=dev`, and this makes the playbook then load a `vars` file it thinks should be located at `/opt/varsfiles/dev.yml`. So we can set specific variable data for different environments (dev, QA, and so on) and reuse our playbooks. Nice, right?

Hosts and Inventory

Ansible offers an inventory system that helps administrators manage the devices they intend to target via Ansible playbook execution or ad hoc command execution. The inventory system allows the administrator to identify inventory items (devices) and group them according to their needs. These inventory items are maintained via Ansible inventory files, which can then be targeted directly via the command line.

Out-of-the-box, Ansible offers a default inventory file, which is typically located in the `/etc/ansible/hosts` file location. If one inventory file is not enough to effectively manage your inventory, additional inventory files can be created and stored either in the same location or in a location of your choosing. When calling the `ansible-playbook` command to invoke Ansible and execute either an ad hoc command or trigger a `playbook run`, Ansible has the `-i` option to allow alternate inventory files to be specified directly on the command line. The following is a set of examples that illustrate targeting inventory files from the command line:

```
# This example uses the default hosts file provided by Ansible
# and executes playbook.yml
$> ansible-playbook -i hosts playbook.yml

# This example specifies an alternative hosts file
# and executes playbook.yml
$> ansible-playbook -i /opt/mynewinventoryfile playbook.yml

# This example specifies a set of hosts directly on the
# command line and executes playbook.yml
$> ansible-playbook -i fqdn.example.com, playbook.yml
```

Now that we have a good idea of how to specify alternate inventory files via the command line, let's take a look at some ways in which we can leverage an Ansible inventory file.

Targeting Infrastructure

When creating automation that is aimed at targeting one or multiple devices, we need a way to instruct Ansible which hosts to target and which playbooks should target which hosts. In order for Ansible to maintain an orderly congregation of hostnames, IP addresses, and domain names, the creators of Ansible have provided an Ansible inventory hosts file and the ability to group and target groups of hosts via Ansible playbooks. Ansible host are generally defined within the Ansible inventory `hosts` file, which is traditionally located at the following file location on the Ansible control server:

```
/etc/ansible/hosts
```

As we mentioned in the previous chapter, the Ansible `hosts` file allows the Ansible developer to maintain a list or set of groups of devices that Ansible can target via playbooks. The way we instruct Ansible to target specific groups of hosts is through the `hosts` line entry within a given Ansible playbook. Let's consider the following hosts groups and Ansible playbook examples:

Ansible hosts file example (`/etc/ansible/hosts`):

```
# Example Ansible hosts file with two defined groups

[WEB]
192.168.10.10
[DATABASE]
192.168.10.11
```

Targeting the `WEB` hosts group via an Ansible playbook (`playbook.yml`):

```
# Example Ansible Playbook, which targets the 'WEB' group
---
- hosts: WEB
  vars :
    http_port : 80
  tasks:
    - name: Install nginx web server
      apt: pkg=nginx state=installed update_cache=true
      notify:
        - start nginx
```

To execute the previous example, simply change into the directory that contains the `playbook.yml` file and execute the following command:

```
# Run Ansible and instruct it to execute the contents of
# playbook.yml against the inventory file of hosts
# (the default Ansible inventory)
$> ansible-playbook playbook.yml -i hosts
```

It is important to understand that Ansible doesn't necessarily need to target an inventory group via the hosts line entry in a playbook. It can also target multiple groups, single hosts, wild cards, and more. Let's take a look at some examples of other ways in which we can input the data within the `hosts` section:

```
# Example hosts line values:

hosts: all -- Applies the current playbook to all hosts in the specified
inventory file
  hosts: hostname -- Applies the playbook ONLY to the specified host
'hostname'
  hosts: groupname -- Applies the playbook to all hosts in specified
groupname
  hosts: groupA,groupB -- Applies the playbook to hosts in groupB and
groupB
  hosts: group1,host1 -- A combination of single hosts and groups
  hosts: *.google.com -- Applies the playbook to wildcard matches
```

In addition to these examples of loose host line values, the `hosts` section can also contain groupings such as these:

```
[WEB]
192.168.10.10
[PRODUCTION]
192.168.10.11
```

In addition to these examples, the `hosts` section can also leverage Ansible variables to target specific hosts. An example of this type of implementation is provided next:

```
hosts: $myhosts -- apply the playbook to all hosts specified in the
variable $myhosts
```

Once the playbook reflects the `$myhosts` variable, we can set that variable with something like the example provided next:

```
$> ansible-playbook playbook.yml --extra-vars="groups=PRODUCTION"
```

Based on this command, we can see that the we are able to target the production group (defined in the previous `hosts` file).

Ansible Modules

Ansible provides a very robust set of tools that can aid immensely in operational implementations. Common operational implementations include managing the configuration of a given system (ensuring that packages are installed, files are present, directory structures exist, and so on), provisioning a given system to meet a set of prerequisites, and more. As we discovered earlier, playbooks and their tasks help us achieve these goals by executing a set of automations against a given system.

While the knowledge we have gained can give us the basics we need to implement simple automations, we have really just barely scratched the surface of how Ansible works. Ansible integrates with hundreds of system-level tasks and thousands of external third-party solutions and can be leveraged in ways we haven't even begun to fathom. Let's peel back the layers a bit and see how we can leverage Ansible for basic Configuration Management.

Ansible provides the bulk of its task functionality through Ansible modules. Ansible modules are essentially standalone interfaces that integrate Ansible with an OS or another technology. For example, Ansible has a module that integrates Ansible playbook automation with JIRA. So the JIRA module provides a direct link between the functionality available via the JIRA API and the automation formatting that makes up an Ansible playbook task.

The Ansible implementation has three different module types. These module types are Core, Curated, Community, and Custom. Each of these modules have their own specific function and role within the Ansible solution. Let's take a minute to look at what the Ansible documentation has to say about these different module types:

- **Core**: These are modules that the core Ansible team maintains and will always ship with ansible itself. They will also receive slightly higher priority for all requests. Non-core modules are still fully usable.

- **Curated**: Some examples of curated modules are submitted by other companies or maintained by the community. Maintainers of these types of modules must watch for any issues reported or pull requests raised against the module.

> Core committers will review all modules becoming curated. Core committers will review proposed changes to existing curated modules once the community maintainers of the module have approved the changes. Core committers will also ensure that any issues that arise due to Ansible engine changes will be remediated. Also, it is strongly recommended (but not presently required) for these types of modules to have unit tests.
> These modules are currently shipped with Ansible, but might be shipped separately in the future.

- **Community**: These modules are not supported by core committers or by companies/partners associated to the module. They are maintained by the community.

> They are still fully usable, but the response rate to issues is purely up to the community. Best effort support will be provided but is not covered under any support contracts.
> These modules are currently shipped with Ansible, but will most likely be shipped separately in the future.

In this section we are going to look at the core module solution and try to understand how it functions and the capabilities that it provides.

At the time of writing, there are 1,021 unique Ansible modules available and provided by Ansible's out-of-the-box solution. This means that Ansible has the potential to integrate very tightly with any number of operating systems, tools, and open source software. To better illustrate this, let's take a quick look at just the categories of the Ansible modules provided at the official documentation (`http://docs.ansible.com/ansible/modules_by_category.html`):

- Cloud modules
- Clustering modules
- Commands modules
- Crypto modules
- Database modules
- Files modules
- Identity modules
- Inventory modules
- Messaging modules
- Monitoring modules
- Network modules
- Notification modules
- Packaging modules
- Remote management modules
- Source control modules
- Storage modules
- System modules
- Utilities modules
- Web infrastructure modules
- Windows modules

As we can see from the list, Ansible's integration is highly robust. Let's explore some of the more common modules and see how we can use them within our playbook tasks.

Managing packages in Ansible

Ansible integrates very tightly with a number of Linux flavors. This integration enables Ansible playbooks to maintain packages on target systems in a succinct and structured manner. From `yum` to `apt` and `opencws`, the package-management solution provided by the Ansible developers is robust and feature-rich. In this section, we will understand the fundamentals of package management through Ansible playbooks.

Yum

Ansible provides a complete yum module, which effectively integrates it with common RHEL implementations of the yum repository system. Through Ansible's yum interface, it is possible to perform almost all yum-related operations. Some examples of Ansibe's yum capabilities include:

- Installing packages
- Removing packages
- Adding repositories
- Managing GPG checks
- Listing packages

Now that we have a good idea of Ansible's yum ninja skills, let's take a look at some basic examples of how to perform operations with yum:

```
- name: install the latest version of Apache
  yum:
    name: httpd
    state: latest
- name: remove the Apache package
  yum:
    name: httpd
    state: absent
- name: install the latest version of Apache from the testing repo
  yum:
    name: httpd
    enablerepo: testing
    state: present
- name: install one specific version of Apache
  yum:
    name: httpd-2.2.29-1.4.amzn1
    state: present
- name: upgrade all packages
  yum:
```

```
      name: '*'
      state: latest
 - name: install the nginx rpm from a remote repo
   yum:
      name:
http://nginx.org/packages/centos/6/noarch/RPMS/nginx-release-centos-6-0.el6
.ngx.noarch.rpm
      state: present
 - name: install nginx rpm from a local file
   yum:
      name: /usr/local/src/nginx-release-centos-6-0.el6.ngx.noarch.rpm
      state: present
 - name: install the 'Development tools' package group
   yum:
      name: "@Development tools"
      state: present- name: install the 'Gnome desktop' environment group
   yum:
      name: "@^gnome-desktop-environment"
      state: present
 - name: List Ansible packages and register result to print with debug
later.
   yum:
      list: ansible
   register: result
```

The apt-get and dpkg

Ansible's integration with apt-get is equally as tight as Ansible's integration with yum. The apt-get package, for those who are not familiar with it, is a package-management solution leveraged by Debian-based operating systems. The implementation of apt-get actuality sits on top of another solution called dpkg, and Ansible provides modules that support both. In this specific section, we will discuss apt-get specifically. In order to better understand the architecture that we are referencing, an illustration is provided next:

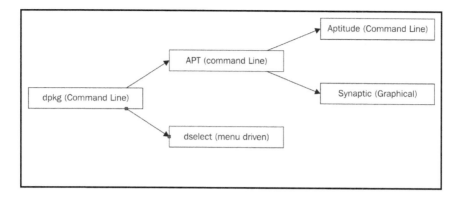

Now that we have a good understanding of how `apt-get` works, let's take a look at some examples of how Ansible integrates with this specific package manager:

```
- name: Update repositories cache and install "foo" package
  apt:
    name: foo
    update_cache: yes

- name: Remove "foo" package
  apt:
    name: foo
    state: absent

- name: Install the package "foo"
  apt:
    name: foo
    state: present

- name: Install the version '1.00' of package "foo"
  apt:
    name: foo=1.00
    state: present

- name: Update the repository cache and update package "nginx" to latest
  version using default release squeeze-backport
  apt:
    name: nginx
    state: latest
    default_release: squeeze-backports
    update_cache: yes

- name: Install latest version of "openjdk-6-jdk" ignoring "install-
  recommends"
  apt:
```

```
        name: openjdk-6-jdk
        state: latest
        install_recommends: no

    - name: Update all packages to the latest version
      apt:
        upgrade: dist

    - name: Run the equivalent of "apt-get update" as a separate step
      apt:
        update_cache: yes

    - name: Only run "update_cache=yes" if the last one is more than 3600
seconds ago
      apt:
        update_cache: yes
        cache_valid_time: 3600

    - name: Pass options to dpkg on run
      apt:
        upgrade: dist
        update_cache: yes
        dpkg_options: 'force-confold,force-confdef'

    - name: Install a .deb package
      apt:
        deb: /tmp/mypackage.deb

    - name: Install the build dependencies for package "foo"
      apt:
        pkg: foo
        state: build-dep

    - name: Install a .deb package from the internet.
      apt:
        deb: https://example.com/python-ppq_0.1-1_all.deb
```

 In addition to `yum` and `apt` integration, Ansible actually integrates very well with a number of additional package-management solutions for other Linux distributions. Each of these (like the previous two) is supported through an Ansible module. The modules for these other flavors of Linux are crafted in such a way so as to provide as robust an integration as possible. For a complete module list of supported package-management solutions, the following link should provide a comprehensive guide:

`http://docs.ansible.com/ansible/list_of_packaging_modules.html`
.

Managing users in Ansible

Managing users within an Ansible playbook need not be a daunting task. Ansible's `user` module set provides tight integration with the Ansible core and the system-level users solution. The Ansible user module provides us with the ability to manage users and user attributes via YAML. As a result, operations such as add, remove, and update are usually quite easy to implement. Let's take a look at how to perform some basic user operations using Ansible in conjunction with the users module:

```
# Create a User 'dortiz'
---
- hosts: all

  tasks:
    - name: Add David Ortiz User to the System
      user:
        name: dortiz
        comment: "David Ortiz has entered the building"

# Create a User 'jdaemon' and add to group baseballplayers
---
- hosts: all

  tasks:
    - name: Add Johnny Daemon User to the System
      user:
        name: jdaemon
        comment: "Johnny Daemon has entered the building"
        groups: baseballplayers
```

For a complete list of parameters that can be passed through the Ansible users module, refer to the official documentation on the users module located at `http://docs.ansible.com/ansible/user_module.html`.

File and directory management in Ansible

Ansible's file module provides integration between Ansible playbooks and the filesystem itself. This enables us to perform directory operations and basic file operations via an Ansible playbook task. In addition to basic **create**, **remove**, **update**, and **delete** (**CRUD**) operations, we can also set permissions, change owners, set group owners, operate on recursive folder trees, and more.

Let's take a look at some examples of basic file and directory management operations using the `file` module:

```
# Create a directory using an Ansible Task

- name: Creates a directory
  file: path=/opt/helloWorld state=directory

# Create a directory using an Ansible Task,
# which is owned by the baseballplayersgroup

- name: Creates a directory
  file: path=/opt/helloWorld state=directory

# Creates a directory owned by the baseballplayers group
# with CHMO 0775 permissions
- name: Creates directory
  file: path=/opt/helloWorld state=directory owner=baseballplayers
group=baseballplayers mode=0775

# Changes the ownership of myconfiguration.conf to
# bob and changes permissions to 0644
- name:
    file:
      path: /opt/myconfiguration.conf
      owner: bob
      group: admin
      mode: 0644
```

These examples provide just a glimpse into file management and Ansible's file module. For a complete list of available options, consult the Ansible documentation located at `http://do cs.ansible.com/ansible/file_module.html`.

Managing services in Ansible

Managing services using Ansible is a breeze. Service management can be a complex operation and is usually highly dependent on the OS and system type. However, with Ansible's service module, we can easily stop, start, and restart services. This integration provides a high level of reliability and abstracts the fundamental OS-level operations that must be performed. Let's take a look at the Ansible `service` module and see its capabilities:

```
# Example action to start service httpd, if not running
- service:
    name: httpd
    state: started
```

```
# Example action to stop service httpd, if running
- service:
    name: httpd
    state: stopped

# Example action to restart service httpd, in all cases
- service:
    name: httpd
    state: restarted

# Example action to reload service httpd, in all cases
- service:
    name: httpd
    state: reloaded

# Example action to enable service httpd, and not touch the running state
- service:
    name: httpd
    enabled: yes

# Example action to start service foo, based on running process
/usr/bin/foo
- service:
    name: foo
    pattern: /usr/bin/foo
    state: started

# Example action to restart network service for interface eth0
- service:
    name: network
    state: restarted
    args: eth0
```

These examples provide us with some insight into Ansible's service control solution and
how to manage services using Ansible playbooks. Now that we have a grasp on that, let's
take a look at how to transfer files using Ansible.

Transferring files in Ansible

Transferring files from the local Ansible control server to a set of target machines is critical for software deployment implementations. Ansible provides a very handy `copy` module that can help us accomplish exactly this. The `copy` module provides a number of handy property knobs, which can further our goal by allowing us to set file permissions, change ownership, decrypt the file, create backups, and more. Let's take a look at how to deliver files from the local Ansible control server over to target machines using the `copy` module:

```
# Example from Ansible Playbooks
- copy:
    src: /srv/myfiles/foo.conf
    dest: /etc/foo.conf
    owner: foo
    group: foo
    mode: 0644

# The same example as above, but using a symbolic mode
# equivalent to 0644
- copy:
    src: /srv/myfiles/foo.conf
    dest: /etc/foo.conf
    owner: foo
    group: foo
    mode: "u=rw,g=r,o=r"

# Another symbolic mode example, adding some permissions
# and removing others
- copy:
    src: /srv/myfiles/foo.conf
    dest: /etc/foo.conf
    owner: foo
    group: foo
    mode: "u+rw,g-wx,o-rwx"

# Copy a new "ntp.conf file into place, backing up the
# original if it differs from the copied version
- copy:
    src: /mine/ntp.conf
    dest: /etc/ntp.conf
    owner: root
    group: root
    mode: 0644
    backup: yes

# Copy a new "sudoers" file into place, after passing
# validation with visudo
```

```
- copy:
    src: /mine/sudoers
    dest: /etc/sudoers
    validate: 'visudo -cf %s'
```

Now that we have a good idea of how Ansible modules work and some implementation details, let's look at how to expand our knowledge and capabilities in developing robust and easy to maintain playbooks.

Summary

This was quite a chapter. And we are nearing the halfway point in our journey through this book. In this chapter, we learned the basic constructs of Ansible playbook files, what YAML is, and the basic idea of how Jinja is incorporated as well. In addition to understanding the basic constructs, we learned how to create Ansible playbook YAML files, how to create and manage inventory files, and so much more. This chapter was quite a ride: acquiring knowledge and implementing it.

In the next chapter, we will look at playbook syntax. This includes roles, includes, playbook directory structures, and loops and blocks. Consider the next chapter to be progression from of this chapter. Let's get started on it then, shall we?

5
Playbooks – Beyond the Fundamentals

In the previous chapter, we outlined and discussed how to construct Ansible playbook's and inventory host files. This knowledge will help us get up and running with Ansible quickly and is a great foundation to build from. We looked at how to leverage these implementations to target groups of infrastructure and began to see some of the power that Ansible provides. While Ansible was designed with simplicity as its core design construct, that does not mean it is not highly scalable and flexible. In many ways, Ansible's real power and scalability comes from its modular design and simplistic implementation standards combined with an effectively customizable playbook and role design pattern.

While the implementations we have learned thus far have their place and purpose (as basic constructs, and foundational elements), can you imagine how hard a 10,000-line single file Ansible playbook would be to create and manage? Or what if half of that playbook were designed to simply setup web servers? Could there be a better way? Absolutely! A better way of implementing and managing playbook's is to use Ansible roles and the includes. These scenarios are where moving beyond a simple single-file playbook becomes a reality.

In this chapter, we are going to expand our Ansible knowledge and learn how to make use of Ansible roles and includes. We will learn how to expand from a single playbook file into a playbook hierarchy structure where multiple files can be combined and reused to provide an **Object Oriented Programming (OOP)** playbook implementation. In addition to learning roles and include, we will also learn how registers and other more advanced playbook structures work. The specific learning objectives of this chapter are as follows:

- Ansible playbook's and Conditional Logic
- Ansible Loops and Iterators
- Ansible Includes
- Ansible Roles
- Ansible Registers
- Error Trapping
- Ansible Handlers

playbook's and Conditional Logic

Ansible provides a nice integrated way of performing conditional operations. That is to say, a task can be executed when a given condition is met. Some examples of this type of requirement might be to only execute a task *if* the target system is Ubuntu or only execute a task *if* the target system has a specific processor architecture.

Ansible supports conditionals through the implementation of the when operator. In this section, we will take a look at how Ansible manages conditionals and tour through an example of managing tasks through a condition. Let's start with this code:

```
# Reboot Debian Flavored Linux Systems using the WHEN operator tasks:
 - name: "Reboot all Debian flavored Linux systems"
   command: /sbin/reboot -t now
   when: Ansible_os_family == "Debian"
```

In this example, we conditionally specify the Debian family as the requirement for the task to run. Simple enough, right? In addition to the example using the Ansible_os_family implementation, we can also specify variable conditions. Variable conditions let us specify that a variable is set or exists as a requirement to executing the Ansible task. Look at another example of a snippet:

```
# Display Hello World to DevOps readers
vars:
  is_enabled: true
tasks:
    - name: "Tell only DevOps People Hello"
      shell: echo "Hello DevOps Readers"
      when: is_enabled
```

In this example, we can see that if the when operator is set to true, we tell the user *hello*. Simple enough logic, right? In addition to this implementation, we can also use the inverse of this logic, that is, to execute a task when the operator is not set. Let's take a look at an example of this in inverse operation in action:

```
tasks:

  - shell: echo "The operator has not been set"
    when: myvar is undefined
```

While simple logic can be implemented using these solutions, oftentimes we need something a bit more comprehensive. In addition to simple logic conditions Ansible provides, we can also perform more complex implementations. One such implementation is the use of iterators and conditions. Let's take a look at an example of how to implement this:

```
# Iterator with conditional logic to stop the iteration at a specified
number

tasks:
  - command: echo {{ item }}
    with_items: [ 1, 2, 3, 4, 5, 6, 7, 8, 9, 10 ]
    when: item > 7
```

In this example, we have a simple command of echo, which takes an iterator array (with_items), and we terminate the loop if the item count gets larger than 7. The output of this example should be similar to the following screenshot:

```
jmcallister@ubuntu:/opt/playbooks$ ansible-playbook -i 'localhost, ' -c local iterator_conditional.y
ml

PLAY ***********************************************************************

TASK [setup] **************************************************************
ok: [localhost]

TASK [command] ************************************************************
skipping: [localhost] => (item=0)
skipping: [localhost] => (item=1)
skipping: [localhost] => (item=2)
skipping: [localhost] => (item=3)
skipping: [localhost] => (item=4)
skipping: [localhost] => (item=5)
changed: [localhost] => (item=6)
changed: [localhost] => (item=7)
changed: [localhost] => (item=8)
changed: [localhost] => (item=9)
changed: [localhost] => (item=10)

PLAY RECAP ****************************************************************
localhost                  : ok=2    changed=1    unreachable=0    failed=0

jmcallister@ubuntu:/opt/playbooks$ _
```

Great! Now that we know how to do this, let's take a look at how to use conditionals based on the output of previous commands. Here is an example:

```
when: "'divide by zero' in output"
```

After the implementation of Ansible 2.0, the kind folks at Ansible provided us with a handy way of adding conditionals to Ansible roles. As a result, we can now use conditional logic directly within our role declarations. This is accomplished via the following syntax:

```
# Conditional Logic directly in the Ansible Roles

- hosts: all
  roles:
    - { role: centos_config, when: Ansible_os_family == 'CentOS' }
```

So we have learned how useful conditionals can be within an Ansible playbook. Now let's move on from conditionals onto iterators and loops. Iterators and loops provide us with a really handy way to reduce the amount of code we write and allow us to perform repetitive operations easily.

Iterators and Loops

In Ansible (and YAML for that matter), there is usually more than one way to accomplish any given automation. Automation actions can be implemented in simple YAML format or can be potentially grouped together by using the `with_items` iterator. In this section, we will take a look at iterators and learn how we can leverage them to reduce the amount of YAML code we need to write and organize our playbook tasks more effectively.

If you are familiar with basic programming concepts, the idea of an iterator is not new or novel. In fact, Ansible supports multiple variations of an iterator: everything from traditional loops to `Do...Until`, numerical iterators, and many more. Iterators in the context of Ansible playbook's are almost identical in nature as traditional programming implementations of iterators, with a few specific syntax caveats.

In this section, we are going to look at the multiple loop variations that Ansible supports. We will begin by looking at standard basic loops and move onto more complex implementations as we progress through this section. Let's get moving!

Basic loops using with_items

Ansible's YAML integration supports a basic loop syntax for reducing duplication in code. This can be especially handy when installing packages, copying files, or managing sets of items. The Ansible implementation of this is managed via the `with_items` iterator. Ansible's `with_items` iterator allows us to specify the task to perform once and a list of items to perform the same task repetitively. Let's look at a comparison of an Ansible task that uses `with_items` and the same set of tasks that does not use this feature:

```
# playbook.yml without list based iterators
---
- hosts: all
  tasks:
    - name: Install Apache2
      apt: name=apache2 state=installed

    - name: Install VIM
      apt: name=vim state=installed

    - name: Install TMUX
      apt: name=tmux state=installed

    - name: Install MOSH
      apt: name=mosh state=installed

# playbook.yml using an Iterator to install packages
---
- hosts: all
  tasks:
    - name: Install list of packages
      apt: name={{item}} state=installed
        with_items:
          - apache2
          - vim
          - tmux
          - mosh
```

Based on this example, we can see that we can alleviate some tedium when writing our playbook's by using a `with_items` iterator. The iterator in this case takes a list of items and then repeats the task any number of times with a different item substituted during each iteration.

In addition to specifying `with_items` directly inline in the task, we can also leverage a list defined within a YAML variables file, or the vars section. This can be accomplished like so:

```
with_items: "{{ myvarlist }}"
```

Nested loops using with_nested

In addition to the simple loops we described previously, Ansible's syntax also supports the idea of nested looping. Nested loops in many ways are similar in nature to a set of arrays that would be iterated over using the `with_nested` operator. Nested loops provide us with a succinct way of iterating over multiple lists within a single task. This could be useful in cases where multiple data items are required (such as creating user accounts with different names and details, or maybe seeding a MySQL database). Let's look at an example:

```
# Demo of Nested Loops Using Ansible. To execute use the following command:
# > Ansible-playbook -i 'localhost,' -c local nested_loops.yml

---
- name: Demo of nested loops using with_nested
  hosts: all
  remote_user: root
  vars:
    listA: [1, 2]
    listB: [a, b]
  tasks:
    - name: Say Hello using Nested Loops
      debug: msg="The values in the array are {{item[0]}} and {{item[1]}}"
      with_nested:
        - listA
        - listB
```

Here is the output from the console when we run this playbook on the command line:

```
                                     Ubuntu Server [Running]
TASK [setup] ********************************************************************
ok: [localhost]

TASK [Say Hello Using nested Loops] ********************************************
ok: [localhost] => (item=[1, u'a']) => {
    "item": [
        1,
        "a"
    ],
    "msg": "The values in the arrays are 1 and a"
}
ok: [localhost] => (item=[1, u'b']) => {
    "item": [
        1,
        "b"
    ],
    "msg": "The values in the arrays are 1 and b"
}
ok: [localhost] => (item=[2, u'a']) => {
    "item": [
        2,
        "a"
    ],
    "msg": "The values in the arrays are 2 and a"
}
ok: [localhost] => (item=[2, u'b']) => {
    "item": [
        2,
        "b"
    ],
    "msg": "The values in the arrays are 2 and b"
}

PLAY RECAP *********************************************************************
localhost                  : ok=2    changed=0    unreachable=0    failed=0

root@ubuntu:/opt/playbooks# _
```

As we can see from this example, we have the ability within our playbook to use arrays and iterate over them by simply referring to them using the `with_items` clause. Neat, right?

Looping over hashes using with_dict

For those of you who are familiar with programming languages, the idea of a hash is nothing new. For those of you who are not familiar, a hash is simply a set of data points identified by a key. Within a hash can be multiple keys, and each key has an associated value.

Let's take a look at a basic example of a hash to get a better idea of how this unique but popular data structure works:

Key	Value
firstName	Bugs
lastName	Bunny
location	Earth

From this, table we can see that a key is simply an identifier, and the value that key represents could be any string or data piece stored in the value table that is associated with that specific key. So how does this apply to Ansible? Ansible provides us a `with_dict` operator, which we can leverage to iterate over key/value pairs. Let's look at an example:

```
# Example of iterating over a YAML dictionary (iterator_keyvalue.yml)
# To execute save this as a YML file and run the following command
# > Ansible-playbook -i 'localhost,' -c local iterator_keyvalue.yml
---
- name: Say Hello to our Favorite Looney Tune Characters
  hosts: all
  vars:
    looney_tunes_characters:
      bugs:
        full_name: Bugs A Bunny
      daffy:
        full_name: Daffy E Duck
      wiley:
        full_name: Wiley E Coyote
  tasks:
    - name: Show Our Favorite Looney Tunes
      debug:
        msg: "Hello there: {{ item.key }} your real name is {{
item.value.full_name }}"
        with_dict: "{{ looney_tunes_charachters }}"
```

This example shows a way to store hash data within an Ansible playbook and then iterate over the results. In this specific case, we iterate over the key, which is our looney's short name, and the associated value, which is the looney's full name. When we run this playbook, the output we will see should be something like the following:

```
TASK [setup] ***********************************************************
ok: [localhost]

TASK [Say Hello to our Favorite Looney Tune Charachters] **************
ok: [localhost] => (item={'value': {u'full_name': u'Daffy E Duck'}, 'key': u'daffy'}) => {
    "item": {
        "key": "daffy",
        "value": {
            "full_name": "Daffy E Duck"
        }
    },
    "msg": "Hello Toon: daffy your real name is Daffy E Duck"
}
ok: [localhost] => (item={'value': {u'full_name': u'Bugs A Bunny'}, 'key': u'bugs'}) => {
    "item": {
        "key": "bugs",
        "value": {
            "full_name": "Bugs A Bunny"
        }
    },
    "msg": "Hello Toon: bugs your real name is Bugs A Bunny"
}
ok: [localhost] => (item={'value': {u'full_name': u'Wiley E Coyote'}, 'key': u'wiley'}) => {
    "item": {
        "key": "wiley",
        "value": {
            "full_name": "Wiley E Coyote"
        }
    },
    "msg": "Hello Toon: wiley your real name is Wiley E Coyote"
}

PLAY RECAP ************************************************************
localhost                  : ok=2    changed=0    unreachable=0    failed=0

root@ubuntu:/opt/playbooks# ansible-playbook -i 'localhost,' -c local iterator_keyvalue.yml
```

So we can see from this screenshot that Ansible will neatly iterate over the data sets we requested and say *hello* to our favorite Looney Tunes character.

Iterating over files using with_file

Ansible's `with_file` operator provides us with a handy way to iterate over the contents of a file. This specific iterator operation provides us with a way to iterate over a single file or multiple files in order. To illustrate how this works, let's look at an example:

- `hello.txt`:

      Hello There:

- `favorite_toons.txt`:

      Bugs Bunny
      Daffy Duck
      Mickey Mouse
      Donald Duck
      Wiley E. Coyote

- `iterator_file_contents.yml`:

```
# Example Playbook which Iterates Over the Contents of Two Files
(iterator_file_contents.yml)
---
- name: Say hello to our favorite Looney Toons
  hosts: all
  tasks:
    - name: Say Hello to Our Favorite Looney Toons
      debug:
        msg: "{{ item }}"
      with_file:
        - hello.txt
        - favorite_toons.txt
```

From this example, we should be able to at this point understand basically what it is trying to accomplish. The first thing it will do is display the contents of hello.txt, and subsequently display the contents of favorite_toons.txt. As such, the output should be similar to the following screenshot:

```
root@ubuntu:/opt/playbooks# ansible-playbook -i 'localhost,' -c local iterator_with_files.yml

PLAY [Say hello to our favorite Looney Toons] ********************************

TASK [setup] ****************************************************************
ok: [localhost]

TASK [Say Hello to Our Favorite Looney Toons] ********************************
ok: [localhost] => (item=Hello There:) => {
    "item": "Hello There:",
    "msg": "Hello There:"
}
ok: [localhost] => (item=Bugs Bunny
Donald Duck
Daffy Duck
Mickey Mouse
Wiley E. Coyote
Mini Mouse) => {
    "item": "Bugs Bunny\nDonald Duck\nDaffy Duck\nMickey Mouse\nWiley E. Coyote\nMini Mouse",
    "msg": "Bugs Bunny\nDonald Duck\nDaffy Duck\nMickey Mouse\nWiley E. Coyote\nMini Mouse"
}

PLAY RECAP *****************************************************************
localhost                  : ok=2    changed=0    unreachable=0    failed=0

root@ubuntu:/opt/playbooks# _
```

From this screenshot, we can see that the playbook which uses nesting outputs the names of our favorite Looney Toons character, prefaced with a greeting.

Iterating over sequential numbers

Counting through a sequential number set is a fundamental programming concept. It involves essentially creating a counter that counts forward or backward sequentially by a given step. That is to say, we can count up or down from a given number using Ansible sequential numerical iterators. We can then pipe the numerical data from Ansible into, say, a shell call or a debug message. Let's take a quick look at a brief example:

```
# Ansible Example provided by Ansible.com
# create some test users
 - user:
```

```
    name: "{{ item }}"
    state: present
    groups: "evens"
with_sequence: start=0 end=32 format=testuser%02x
```

The do until iterator

The `Do...Until` iterator has been around for a long time in many programming languages. It is probably one of the most widely implemented iterators that exist. This specific iteration solution provides the developer with the ability to continuously loop through a sequence of code until a specific condition or flag is met. Let's look at a traditional programming example of a `Do...Until` loop versus an Ansible implementation of the same operator:

- VB.NET example:

```
' This example is a VB.NET example of a Do Loop
Do
        Debug.Write("Counter: " & index.ToString)
        index += 1
Loop Until index > 5
```

- Ansible `Do...Until` example:

```
- action:
    /usr/bin/tail -n 1 /var/log/auth.log
  register: result
  until: result.stdout.find("Cannot create session") != -1
  retries: 100
  delay: 1
```

This Ansible `Do` example shows how to tail a log and wait for a specific text to appear. This can be really handy when waiting for a system to spin up or an execution to throw something in a log file.

Iterating over inventory hosts using play_hosts

Inventory hosts are data items too! Each hostname defined within an inventory file can be iterated upon. This implementation of the kind folks at Ansible can be really handy for performing numerous configuration operations, installation items, and much more. In this section, we will look at how to effectively iterate through an inventory file and perform an operation with the hosts defined. The easiest way to iterate through the inventory is to use the play_hosts variable in conjunction with with_items. While this may be the easiest method, it is not the only way to achieve this type of iteration. Let's get started by looking at an example of the play_hosts variable in action:

- hosts.yml:

```
[webserver]
192.168.10.10
192.168.10.11
192.168.10.12

[dbserver]
192.168.30.1
192.168.30.2
192.168.30.3
```

- iterating_inventory_ex1.yml:

```
# Example of a playbook, which iterates over the inventory list.
# Specifically this will display
# all hosts in the webserver group. This example uses the play_hosts
# variable in conjunction
# with with_items to provide an elegant mechanism for iterating.

---
-
  hosts: webserver
  name: "Iteration Example using With_Items and Play_Hosts"
  tasks:
    -
      debug: ~
      msg: "Host Identified: {{ item }}"
      with_items:
        - "{{ play_hosts }}"
```

This example shows the user a list of all hosts that are currently targeted by the execution, in this case, the items in the webserver group.

In addition to the previously shown example, which uses the `play_hosts` variable, we can also implement a similar solution using Ansible group identifiers. Group identifiers are a neat way to access the data (hosts in our case) that Ansible is using as part of this specific run. This implementation is actually in some ways slightly more powerful. The power of this solution comes from the key/value pair definition we can specify in the groups variable. Let's take a look at an example of how we can use group identifiers to effect the same output as the previous example:

```
# Display inventory using groups['webserver']
- debug:
    msg: "{{ item }}"
  with_items:
    - "{{ groups['webserver'] }}"
```

As we can see from this example, we can not only target the current hosts targeted by the play, but also any specific group defined within the inventory. For example, we can fetch a list of *all* hosts by simply specifying `{{ groups['all'] }}`. Or if we wanted to target only the `dbserver` group, we could do something like this:

```
with_items:
    - "{{ groups['dbserver'] }}"
```

Includes

It is completely feasible to create a playbook as a single small or large file. Many new Ansible developers actually begin developing playbook's this way, and generally, this implementation methodology is a perfectly normal way to initially learn Ansible playbook creation. Sooner or later though, learning to reuse portions of a playbook will become something very useful and will help better organize playbook development efforts.

On a fundamentally simplistic level, using an Ansible include statement allows us to reuse positions of our automation in one or multiple locations. Consider this in some ways like a method or function in programming that we can execute over and over, essentially allowing us to write the automation once and then reuse it many times.

This is a far more effective way to reuse automation as it removes the need for repeating the creation of various portions of an automation or configuration management solution. As a result, we can begin to think outside of the scope of *step one, step two*—type automation and instead start thinking in terms of *provision this as a web server, or provision this as a web and database server*.

This is a pretty critical concept. We might have a top level playbook that is nothing than a series of includes that are easy to understand and reusable. For example:

- ● - include: add_users.yml
- ● - include: install_httpd.yml
- ● - include: configure_apache.yml
- ● - include: setup_firewall.yml

This is the real power of ansible because the first and last steps there would be executed on every box.

Play-level includes

One of the most effective ways to modularize and organize an Ansible playbook is to use Ansible `include`. Ansible play includes provide an easy way to embed `play` from other YAML files. This implementation allows us to effectively modularize our playbook's automation. Let's take a look at how to leverage a `play` include within an Ansible playbook:

```
# This is an example of a 'play' include, which includes the contents of
playlevelplays.yml

- include: playlevelplays.yml
- name: some play
  hosts: all
  tasks:
    - debug: msg=hello


# This is an example of the contents of playlevelplays.yml

- name: some additional play
  hosts: all
  tasks:
    - debug: msg=hello I am an included file
```

In this example, we can see that to implement a `play` include, we can simply add a - `include: <filename>` directive within our playbook, which will embed the contents of an external Ansible playbook (its plays) into the current playbook and execute those contents at the appropriate step. Neat, right? So to sum up, let's define an Ansible `play` include succinctly: a play-level include allows us to embed additional Ansible plays from external files within our playbook's using the -`include` directive.

In addition to the *vanilla* implementation of Ansible includes we just looked at, the Ansible `include` directive provides us with the ability to pass parameters to our included files upon execution. This can be handy for handing off variables to the other YAML files we include. Let's take a look at how to pass parameters using the `include` directive. An example is provided next:

```
tasks:
  - include: myincludedplaybook.yml user=dbuser
```

Based on the previous example, we can then wield the variable within the target included file using the following syntax `{{user}}`. So a more complete example might look like the following:

```
tasks:
  - include: myincludedplaybook.yml user=dbuser

  - debug:
    msg: "System {{ user }} user is AWESOME!"
```

Now that we have a grasp of play-level includes, let's take a look at task includes.

Task-level includes

In addition to play includes, Ansible supports an additional implementation of the `include` directive. The second implementation is called a **task include**. Task includes are different from `play` includes, in that the contents of the included file would only be a YAML file containing a static list of tasks to execute. To implement a task include, we must specify the include directive at the task level. Let's take a look at an example of a task include solution:

```
# This is an example of a 'play' include

- include: myplaybook.yml
- name: some play
  hosts: all
  tasks:
    - debug: msg=hello

    # An Example of a task level include
    - include: additionaltasks.yml
```

From this example, we can see the `include` statement provided would include the contents of the file `additionaltasks.yml`. The important thing to understand here is scope. Play-level includes will need to have a complete play or set of plays within, whereas `task` includes should only have a YAML-formatted list of tasks. Let's look at an example of each for a bit of clarity. Consider the following two files, adequately named `additionaltasks.yml`.

The content of `additionaltasks.yml` is illustrated here:

```
---
# additional_tasks.yml example
- name: some task
  command: /bin/ls
- name: some other tasks
  command: /bin/ps -ef
```

So now, we know that Ansible supports two scopes of the `include` directive: the first imports a set of plays, and the second imports a set of tasks. These two distinctions are important to understand as they are a powerful feature that can be used to modularize automation and configuration management implementations. By effectively using includes, we can create highly feature-rich automation and configuration management solutions without redundancy in code.

 As of Ansible 2, you can develop unlimited levels of includes. This means that one file can include another, and within the second, you can include additional ones. There is no limit to the number of includes supported.

Dynamic includes

In conjunction with the two basic include types that we mentioned before, Ansible 2.0 supports dynamic task-level includes. A dynamic include is simply a variable translation support within an `include`. As a result of this implementation, we should note that the inclusion is not actually evaluated by Ansible until the moment it is set to be executed. This allows adding variables within an include, which was not possible prior to Ansible 2.0. This implementation can more specifically leverage loops and variable use within the `include` statement. This additional functionality provides us with a significant amount of flexibility within our playbook. Let's take a look at a few examples of **dynamic includes**:

```
# A basic dynamic include using a variable
- include: "{{dbserver}}.yml"
```

This example shows us that it is possible to use variable names within our `include` statement. This can be useful for dynamically specifying the file to include, or having the `include` file be assigned at runtime. Beyond this implementation, we can also use dynamic includes to pass a list of variables between the master playbook and child. An example of this is provided next:

```
# Dynamic include with parameters as a loop
- include: myplaybook.yml param={{item}}
  with_items:
  - apples
  - oranges
  - {{favorite_fruit}}
```

From this example, we can see we are passing `apples`, `oranges`, and the variable `{{favorite_fruit}}` to our included playbook using the `with_items` notation (more on this later). This should give you a pretty good idea of how to pass information from one playbook to an include file.

Now that we have a pretty good grasp of how Ansible can be more dynamic, let's take a look at Ansible roles and see how those fit into our implementations and development efforts.

Ansible Roles

Ansible works very well with supporting a single-file 10,000-line long playbook (please don't actually do that). However, when playbook's grow out of control, Ansible provides a very nice way to break automation into multiple files (as illustrated before using includes). Yet, as we start to grow the number of files we need to include, things can become hairy to manage and maintain. So what is an Ansible developer to do? Roles to the rescue! Ansible roles provide us with a really unique way of dividing out our automation into uniquely defined responsibilities.

In addition to providing configuration management modularization, Ansible roles provide us with a best-practice approach to organizing automation within a playbook and developing reusable solutions. The Ansible *roles* implementation simply represents an automated, well-structured implementation of an Ansible includes solution (which we discussed in the previous section). This means that the include directives are already defined and implemented so long as the predefined directory structure is honored within the roles implementation.

So to sum up, let's consider the following definition for Ansible roles:

A role is a set of Ansible tasks or configuration management automation grouped by a common purpose or responsibility.

To begin understanding how Ansible roles work on a fundamental level, it is probably best to start with a simple flat-file Ansible playbook that installs and configures a LAMP server (Linux, Apache, MySQL, and PHP) and then implement the same solution using Ansible roles and look at the implementation differences. This will give us a good apples-to-apples comparison of how roles implementations differ from standard playbook's and how to organize the responsibilities. For this tutorial, we will be using an Ubuntu-based Ansible control server. Let's get started:

The content of `AnsibleLAMPwithoutRoles.yml` is illustrated here:

```
# playbook.yml
---
- hosts: all
  tasks:
    - name: Install Apache
      apt: name=apache2 state=present

    - name: Install PHP module for Apache
      apt: name=libapache2-mod-php5 state=present

    - name: Install PHP
      apt: name=libapache2-mod-php5 state=present

    - name: Install MySQL
      apt: name=libapache2-mod-php5 state=present

    - name: 3. start Apache
      service: name=apache2 state=running enabled=yes

    - name: 4. install Hello World PHP script
      copy: src=index.php dest=/var/www/index.php
```

Based on this playbook, we can see we are instructing Ansible to install and configure a basic LAMP solution via a single playbook. This includes installing Apache2, PHP, MySQL, and so on. With Ansible roles, we can accomplish the same tasks with a bit more elegance and modularity.

As mentioned earlier, Ansible roles are basically include statements that are pre-baked into the Ansible implementation based on a set of predefined directory structures. Let's take a look at this same basic configuration management implementation and how the directory structure that makes up Ansible roles would need to be applied. On your local system, replicate the following directory and file structure (leave the file contents blank for the moment):

Once the directory and file structure have been created, the next thing we need to fill in is the top-level `playbook.yml` file, which we will use to specify the roles we want and execute them. Here is the content to add to `playbook.yml`:

```
# playbook.yml
---
- hosts: all
  roles:
    - webserver
    - dbserver
```

The purpose of this file is to simply act as a pointer to the roles we wish to execute as part of our Ansible run. The `roles` defined within in this case are a `webserver` role and a `dbserver` role. Each role will be defined by naming and folder convention. Let's move on to the roles themselves. In our example, we have two task files that need to be created/modified (the `webserver` tasks file and the `dbserver` tasks file). These are respectively named `main.yml` and reside in the tasks folder. Let's fill in each. The contents for each are provided next.

The content of `webserver/tasks/main.yml` and `dbserver/tasks/main.yml` is illustrated here:

```
# roles/dbserver/tasks/main.yml

- name: Install Mysql Server Packages
  yum: name={{ item }} state=installed
  with_items:
   - mysql-server
   - MySQL-python
- name: Start Mysql Service
  service: name=mysqld state=started enabled=yes

- name: Create Example Database
  mysql_db: name=foo state=present

- name: Create Example DB User
  mysql_user: name=foo password=bar priv=*.*:ALL host='%' state=present
```

```
# roles/webserver/tasks/main.yml
---
- name: Install Apache HTTPD Server Packages
  yum: name={{ item }} state=installed
  with_items:
   - httpd

- name: Start Http Service
  service: name=http state=started enabled=yes
```

When we run this playbook with our roles defined, we can see that Ansible understands how to traverse the main playbook and execute the roles required to ensure that Apache and MySQL are properly installed and running.

Ansible Register Variables

Ansible registers provide us with a nice way of capturing the results of a given task and executing a set of additional automations based on the captured results. In many ways, this is similar to variable declarations, although registers are more global in nature. Ansible registers provide us with a way of storing this captured data for later and then conditionalizing future tasks based on the results of previous ones.

Simple Ansible registers

The most basic Ansible register implementations require us to only `register` the output of a given operation. An example of how to define a simple register is provided next:

```
---
- name: A Simple Ansible Register Example
  hosts: all
  tasks:
      - shell: tail -n 100 /etc/motd
        register: motd_contents
```

In this example, we use the register operator to capture the last 100 lines of the system's MOTD file and store it in a global `register` variable, `motd_contents`. Ansible registers essentially create a new Ansible fact at runtime, which can be then used later within the play as part of a conditional.

But how exactly do we leverage stored registers later? Good question! Let's explore.

Accessing registers

Accessing Ansible registers later within the same `play` as they were created can be accomplished fairly easily: all we need to do is use the the `when` conditional. We learned about the basics of how to leverage the `when` conditional earlier in this chapter. But in this context it lets us access registers. Let's look at an example of how to use the `when` conditional to access our `register`:

```
---
- name: A Simple Ansible Register Example
  hosts: all
  tasks:
      - shell: tail -n 100 /etc/motd
        register: motd_contents

    - shell: echo "Our MOTD file contains the word Bugs Bunny"
        when: motd_contents.stdout.find('bugs bunny') != -1
```

The important line in this playbook is the `when` line (obviously). The interesting portion of it is the idea of `.stdout.find`, which is attached to the end of our register variable. This extension in many ways looks like a set of OOP methods. That would be an accurate way to identify those specific calls.

In our example, we told Ansible to look at the contents of STDOUT (standard command-line output) and find a specific text. If Ansible were able to properly find the text, only then would the task have been executed. Nifty, right?

Additional conditional logic with registers

Ansible registers are not limited only by the find method of STDOUT. In addition to basic search criteria, we can also apply many other comparisons. In this section, we will identify the more common methods that can be attached to a register variable and learn what other comparisons we can perform.

Null or empty comparisons

Null or empty string comparisons are common in most programming languages, and Ansible is no different. Applying a null or empty string check to an Ansible register can be accomplished via the following solution:

```
when: <registername>.stdout == ""
```

In addition to this specific implementation, we can also apply other variables to our conditionals with registers. Let's see how.

Vars and Ansible registers

Ansible registers also support the use of regular predefined variable comparisons within an Ansible register when clause. This implementation lets us say something like the following:

```
"when varfoo is in register, execute the task"
```

This plain English comparison could be represented in Ansible YAML form via something like this:

```
with_items: varfoo.stdout.find("{{bar}}") > 0
```

This conditional simply specifies that if the contents of varfoo exist within the stdout of register varfoo, then execute the task.

Iterating over register contents

Finally, the contents of the register can be iterated over to create new things and adapt existing system solutions. This type of implementation might be something like creating a list of directories, touching a set of files, or creating a list of users. Basically, it means we can use the contents of the register as a list. Let's take a look at a quick example provided by `htt ps://www.Ansible.com/`:

```
--
- name: registered variable usage as a with_items list
  hosts: all

  tasks:

    - name: retrieve the list of home directories
      command: ls /home
      register: home_dirs

    - name: add home dirs to the backup spooler
      file: path=/mnt/bkspool/{{ item }} src=/home/{{ item }} state=link
      with_items: "{{ home_dirs.stdout_lines }}"
      # same as with_items: "{{ home_dirs.stdout.split() }}"
```

Based on this example, we can see that our `with_items` clause is now used to create a set of files and folders. However, the `home_dirs` variable is set through a register instead of a standard Ansible variable.

Ansible Handlers

Ansible handlers by default are run at the end of the actual execution of a playbook. They are different from registers in that they provide us with a way of creating a set of automation that can be executed once (and only once) at the end of a playbook based on a set of conditions provided during the execution. Logically, this could look something like the following:

- Run role `foo`
- Run role `bar`:
    - If role `bar`'s service start failed, trigger a flag
- Execute handlers:
    - If a trigger was flagged, do something

While this example may seem similar in some ways to conditionals, it is in many ways very different. That is to say, the handler would only get executed the one time regardless of how many times the flag was tripped. In addition, the other variance would be that a handler is more global in nature. That is to say, regardless of which role tripped the flag of the handler, it would still get executed, thus making the solution non-modular.

Confused? Let's take a look at an example of an Ansible handler:

```
--
- name: Example Handler
  hosts: all
  tasks:
    - command: service httpd restart
      notify: restart service

    - command: service mysqld restart
      notify: restart service

    - command: service cron.d restart
      notify: restart service

    - command: service iptables restart
      notify: restart service

  handlers:
    - name: restart service
      include: tasks/restart_verify.yml
```

From this example, we can see we have two new concepts: the `notify` operator and the `handlers` operator. Notify in some ways represents a global event system, which throws an event out when triggered. The handlers on the other hand represent listeners to those events.

So essentially, we can use the `notify` solution to trigger a set of tasks downstream after the main playbook has completed its execution. Nice, right?

Summary

In this chapter, we discovered a number of new techniques of developing and managing playbook's. We learned how to leverage `includes` to modularize our playbook structures and provide us with a level of reusability within our implementations. We learned how to implement conditional logic within our playbook's. We found out how to deal with iterators and loops. We discovered how to implement roles in Ansible and how we can use this structure to organize and better manage complex configuration management and automation tasks. We learned how to best organize our playbook's for reusability. We learned how handlers and registers work and discovered ways we can make our automation solutions more fault tolerant, and we discussed how to effectively enforce basic configuration management implementations.

This information represents the basic cursory information you will need to become a successful Ansible developer and pave the way for success in configuration management. To assist you on your way, the `https://www.Ansible.com/` documentation can be of great use. As such, this resource should become your go-to guide for all things Ansible related.

In the next chapter, we will discover Jinja2. Jinja provides Ansible with a huge amount of flexibility as it allows conditionals, loops, variables, and so much more. By the time we complete the next chapter, we should have a pretty good idea of how we can develop playbook's and leverage Jinja to support our implementations.

6
Jinja in Ansible

JINJA was created in 2008 by Armin Ronacher and aims to replace similar template engines with a more modern and structured solution. Jinja was designed for Python (the programming language that Ansible was created with) and, coupled with Ansible, to provide a framework that integrates seamlessly with YAML. Ansible's YAML implementation and programmatic playbook solution incorporates this robust Jinja template engine. Like many other template solutions (Django, Smarty, and so on), Jinja was designed to provide structural support for reusable text with context specific alterations (environments, hosts, and so on) and comprehensive functionality that developers have come to rely on.

For those who have experience with Smarty or Django-styled tempting solutions, Jinja will indeed be familiar. The design of the Jinja template solution aims to provide support for designers, developers, and operators alike by providing the ability to add conditional logic, iterative behaviors, and logic oriented solutions while adhering to Python best practices. This solution is particularly useful for playbook developers because it provides a highly adaptive programmatic flexibility that can be leveraged by organizations using environments that are similar in nature but have slight differences. Suffice to say, the initial learning curve of Jinja is low and the usefulness of the markup and logic is high.

In this chapter, we will learn how Ansible integrates with Jinja and how Jinja can be leveraged to provide advanced functionality within Ansible playbook's. We will discover how Jinja came about, see how it can be leveraged to create comprehensive playbook implementations, learn how its syntax cohabitates with Ansible's YAML playbook syntax, and see how Jinja complements Ansible's playbook implementation. By the end of this chapter, we will have covered the following:

- Introduction to Jinja.
- How is Jinja2 used by Ansible?
- Jinja programming constructs.

- Applying Jinja to Ansible playbooks.
- How to create loops and iterators in Jinja2.
- How to make and use Jinja2 template files.
- How to use data structures with Jinja2.

Let's begin, shall we?

Introducing Jinja

Jinja is a templating engine that was developed in 2008 by Armin Ronacher in an effort to provide Python developers with a framework that would supply comprehensive Python-like syntax that could be used within strings and data documents. The solution was designed with similar solutions such as Smarty and Django in mind. Jinja executes its template translations in a sandbox (isolated from the rest of the program execution) so as to prevent the template engine from interfering with the normal operational execution of the Python program.

Jinja2 represents the second major version of the Jinja Python library. Jinja is leveraged to generate string-based documents based on one or more predefined templates (also made of strings). As of the writing of this book, Jinja is in use by numerous open source solutions that are actively developed with Python. Some notable examples of solutions that use Jinja include Salt, Flask, and Ansible.

When coupled with Ansible and YAML, Jinja adds significant amounts of power to the Ansible playbook architecture. Jinja in this context provides Ansible playbook developers with the ability to add programming constructs (including variables, conditional logic, loops, and more) to a playbook and structure it in such a way where it can be leveraged as a complete programming solution for automation. Before we get ahead of ourselves and start looking at all the neat stuff that Jinja can do, let's first understand how it actually works.

Jinja is a software solution designed to combine templates with a data model to produce result documents. The templates contain special markup tags and logic that are parsed and logically combined during the execution of the template-parsing process.

To better explain the concept of a template engine, the following Python code shows a basic example of string manipulation using Jinja:

Basic Jinja Python implementation:

```
# A Simple Jinja Python Template example from jinja2 import Template

exampleJinjaTemplate = Template('Hello {{ place }}!')
exampleJinjaTemplate.render(place='World')

>>>Output: 'Hello World!'
```

From the example we just saw, we can observe that this simple Python script does the following:

1. Imports the Jinja template engine library.
2. Defines a simple string template, `['Hello {{ place }] ']`.
3. Renders the template and substitutes the `{{ place }}` tag with the word `World`.

 If you are planning on implementing Jinja directly within Python, the Python Jinja module must be installed within Python first. This can be performed fairly easily, and the instructions on how to do this are readily available at the following URL:

`http://jinja.pocoo.org/docs/2.9/intro/#installation`

The output of the previous example is `Hello World`. From this example, we can observe that the Jinja template tag `{{ ... }}` is translated during the rendering process, whereas the rest of the string-based document is left intact.

Now that we have a pretty good idea of the basic concepts surrounding Jinja, let's take a look at a more realistic example of Jinja in action by looking at a simple Ansible playbook that uses Jinja.

The content of the `playbook.yml` is illustrated as follows:

```
# Example Ansible Jinja2 Template
- hosts:  all
  vars:
    my_var: 'Hello'
    my_var2: 'World'
  tasks:
    - name: Simple Ansible MOTD Template Example
      template:
        src: motdexample.j2
        dest: /etc/motd
        mode: 0777
```

`motdexample.j2`: This is a Jinja2-generated **motd** file also known as **message of the day**. The following content tags will be replaced by the variable data we defined in our playbook (`my_var` and `my_var2`, respectively):

```
Welcome to your System:
{{ my_var }}
{{ my_var2 }}
```

Can you guess what this example will do when executed using Ansible with the assistance of the Jinja2 templating engine? Ansible in conjunction with Jinja will copy the motd file to the target hosts *and* replace the `{{}}` styled variables at the same time with the contents of `my_var` and `my_var2`. Let's take a look at the output of the motd file on the target host:

`/etc/motd` content: This is a Jinja2-generated motd file. The following content tags will be replaced by the variable data we defined in our playbook (`my_var` and `my_var2`, respectively):

```
Welcome to your System:
Hello
World
```

In the context of an Ansible playbook, Jinja allows us to add the `{...}` style tags within our playbook (or within a templated file as we just saw), and Ansible will tell the Jinja library to translate the tags and generate a new document prior to execution. This means we can add common programming constructs either directly to our playbooks or to templated files and make our automation significantly more intelligent. While this example may not seem all that useful, the Jinja implementation overall provides a significant enhancement when coupled with Ansible and YAML.

Consider this implementation for when it is necessary to generate, say, Apache configuration files or MySQL queries. We could although arduously generate each config manually, *or* we could template the content of these and have Ansible iterate. In the coming sections, we will take a deep dive into Jinja programming constructs and learn how to leverage Jinja effectively.

Jinja2 Programming Constructs

Jinja2 was incorporated into the Ansible architecture back in 2012 when Ansible 0.5 was released. The implementation of Ansible at the time incorporated the concept of Jinja2 filters and supported basic Jinja2 syntax. As ansible evolved, so did its developer support for Jinja. By coupling YAML and Jinja2, Ansible was soon able to provide a comprehensive scripting-oriented solution for Ansible playbook developers.

By the time Ansible 1.0 was released, the Ansible playbook concept (including Jinja and YAML) had evolved enough to support a wide array of syntax implementations. As a result of the integration of YAML, Jinja and Ansible's popularity skyrocketed. After the release of Ansible 1.0, playbooks could be authored to incorporate the following syntaxes:

Jinja tag syntax:

```
{{ .. }} for expressions (including variables)
{% ... %} for control structures
{# ... #}} Comments
```

Each of these tags serves a unique role within the Jinja universe, and it is important to understand each completely (so as not to mix them up). In the coming sections, we will learn about these special tags and learn how they can be leveraged to enhance our playbook logic. By the time we're done, we should have a solid understanding of how to wield Jinja implementations of expressions, control statements, and comments.

Expressions, filters, and variables

Jinja filters (also known as **variable expressions**) are very similar in nature to programming variables, although with a key difference. Filter expressions represent a data value item *or* the computed value of a data point in conjunction with another data source. Expressions are evaluated at runtime and can provide a level of flexibility for playbook and template developers. The syntax of Jinja2's expression format is shown as follows:

```
# Basic Syntax of a Jinja Filter or Variable
{{ var | operation expression }}
```

The source data for the `var` section can be from multiple different places. Within an Ansible playbook, there are presently four unique methods for sourcing variable values and content within the context of Jinja:

1. Pass a YAML or JSON file with the `--var-file` option.
2. Create environment variables.
3. Add a top-level defaults section to the playbook.
4. Capture the value from `stdout`.

As we can see from the example syntax we just looked at, Jinja expressions provide significant power that can be now wielded by Ansible playbook developers. Let's take a look at a more comprehensive playbook example using Ansible and Jinja2 expressions.

`playbook.yml`:

```
# Example playbook using simple JINJA2 variable substitution
--
- hosts: 127.0.0.1
  user: root
  vars:
    motd: 'Welcome to your Linux Box'
  tasks:
    - name: Update the /etc/motd
      copy: content='{{motd}}' dest='/etc/motd' force='yes'
```

When we run the playbook, Ansible's output looks like the following screenshot:

Output (contents of `/etc/motd`):

```
Welcome to your Linux Box
```

In this example, we simply set the content of the MOTD file using a basic variable. Simple enough, right? But the real power of Jinja expressions comes when we realize we can source the variable data from multiple sources and perform operations on the variable inline and in real time.

Jinja string concatenation and manipulation

Jinja provides an excellent solution for manipulating strings and concatenating text (joining it with other text). For example, we might want to create a unique MOTD file by adding some additional information to the MOTD contents based on perhaps the hostname. This could be easily achieved via the following ansible playbook and Jinja syntax.

`playbook.yml`:

```
# Example playbook using simple JINJA2 variable substitution
- hosts: 127.0.0.1
  user: root
  vars:
    motd: "Welcome to your Linux Box! You are connected to {{
inventory_hostname_short }}"
  tasks:
    - name: Update the /etc/motd
      copy: content='{{motd}}' dest='/etc/motd' force='yes'
```

As we can see, the example shows how easy it is to concatenate string variables using Jinja. While the example we just looked at is useful, the expression implementation of Jinja is not limited to simple string concatenation. We can also manipulate strings using Jinja. For example, we might use any of the following solutions:

To use *regular expressions* within a Jinja variables:

```
# convert "ansible" to "able"
{{ 'ansible' | regex_replace('^a.*i(.*)$', 'a\\1') }}

# convert "foobar" to "bar"
{{ 'foobar' | regex_replace('^f.*o(.*)$', '\\1') }}

# convert "localhost:80" to "localhost, 80" using named groups
{{ 'localhost:80' | regex_replace('^(?P<host>.+):(?P<port>\\d+)$',
'\\g<host>, \\g<port>') }}

# convert '^f.*o(.*)$' to '\^f\.\*o\(\.\*\)\$'
{{ '^f.*o(.*)$' | regex_escape() }}
```

To convert Jinja variables to *upper* and *lower* case:

```
Uppercase a Variable:

{{ var|upper }}

Lowecase a Variable:

{{ var|lower }}
```

In addition to string manipulation, the Jinja implementation is *far* more powerful. We can also perform math operations using Jinja. Let's learn how.

Basic arithmetic operations in Jinja

In addition to basic string concatenation, we can also perform math and computational operations in Jinja. For example, we can add numerical values together using the following syntax:

```
var: 1
incremented_var: "{{ var + 1 }}"
```

The resulting output would have been calculated as *1+1 = 2*, thus resulting in *2* as the value of the `incremented_var` variable. In conjunction with basic addition, we can also perform multiplication, subtraction, division, and more. A complete list of the basic math operations available is provided next:

```
# Computational operations using Jinja2

Addition Operator: +
Example: {{ var + 1 }}

Subtraction Operator: -
Example: {{ var - 1 }}

Multiplication Operator: *
Example: {{ var * 2 }}

Division Operator: /
Example {{ var / 2 }}
```

From what we just saw, it is easy to see how Jinja can perform basic math operations. But it's not limited to just simple math.

Compound math equations and order of operations in Jinja

Basic operations such as adding, subtracting, multiplying, and dividing can also be combined to create more robust calculated results. This is implemented via the () ordering of operations solution, which is common across many programming languages. It basically states that mathematical operations contained within the parentheses will be performed first with precedence of multiplication, division, addition, and then subtraction. Once the items inside a given set of parentheses are complete, the logic moves outward. An example of this is provided here:

```
Example Math Equation:
2 * (1 + 1)

Order of Operations:
1 + 1 = 2
2 * 2 = 4

Example Math Equation #2:
(( 1 + 2 ) * 3 ) / 2

Order of Operations:
1 + 2 = 3
3 * 3 = 9
9 / 2 = 4.5
```

Within the context of a Jinja expression, this math operation would look something like the following:

```
my_var = "{{ (( 1 + 2 ) * 3) /2 }}"
```

Filters available

Jinja2 is not limited to strictly computational operations. It can be leveraged for any number of operational tasks. Ansible has kindly also provided a number of handy filters, which can be applied to our variable implementations.

The following is a table with a set of examples for the more popular operational tasks one might need to perform using Jinja filter expressions:

Expression name	Example	Description of the expression
`to_json`	`{{ some_variable	to_json }}`	Converts the variable data into JSON format and renders it.
`to_yaml`	`{{ some_variable	to_yaml }}`	Converts the variable data into YAML format and renders it.
`mandatory`	`{{ variable	mandatory }}`	Makes the variable declaration and setting mandatory for the playbook to execute properly.
`default value`	`{{ some_variable	default(5) }}`	Sets a default value for the variable if it is not defined.
`min|max`	`{{ [3, 4, 2]	max }}`  `{{ [3, 4, 2]	min }}`	Fetches the minimum or maximum value from an array. In this case, the values would be 2 or 4, respectively.

`random`	`"{{ ['a','b','c']|random }}"`
	`"{{ 59 |random}} * * * * root /script/from/cron"`
	`"{{ 59 |random(seed=inventory_hostname) }} * * * * root /script/from/cron"`
		Fetches a random item from a list, a random number, or seed value, respectively.

Shuffle	`{{ ['a','b','c']|shuffle }}`
	`# => ['c','a','b']`
	`{{ ['a','b','c']|shuffle }}`
	`# => ['b','c','a']`
		Generates a new random list from an existing random list.

Math log	`{{ myvar	log }}` `{{ myvar	log(10) }}`	Log algorithm math function and log numeric algorithm, respectively.
Square root	`{{ myvar	root }}` `{{ myvar	root(5) }}`	Square root math.
IPV filter	`{{ myvar	ipv4 }}` `{{ myvar	ipv6 }}`	Tests whether a string is a specific IPV version.
Quote filter	`- shell: echo {{ string_value	quote }}`	Wraps the expression evaluated in quotes.

Concatenate lists	`{{ list	join(" ") }}`	Joins list items into a single unified string.
Basename	`{{ path	basename }}`	Linux path basename. Gets `foo.txt` out of `/etc/bar/foo.txt`, for example.
WIN basename	`{{ path	win_basename }}`	Same as basename but for MS Windows.

Now that we have a good understanding of how Ansible and Jinja leverage filters, let's move on to control structures.

 For a complete list of available filters and expressions, consult the official Ansible 2.0 documentation provided at `http://docs.ansible.com/ansible/playbooks_filters.html#filters-for-formatting-data`.

Conditional logic (if-then-else)

Control structures within any programming language provide a way of defining paths for an executing program to flow through based on a condition. In addition to conditional logic, control structures also provide us with a way of repeating like tasks without duplicating code. This is commonly known as **conditional logic and looping**, respectively. Jinja provides us with a set of operators that allow us to loop or conditionally execute code. In this section, we will discuss conditional logic specifically and learn how to leverage it within the context of Jinja.

A conditional statement provides the developer with a way of conditionalizing a sequence of events based on the evaluation of an expression. In most languages, this is accomplished through an if...then-styled solution. Take for example the following flowchart that illustrates the basic principles of conditional logic:

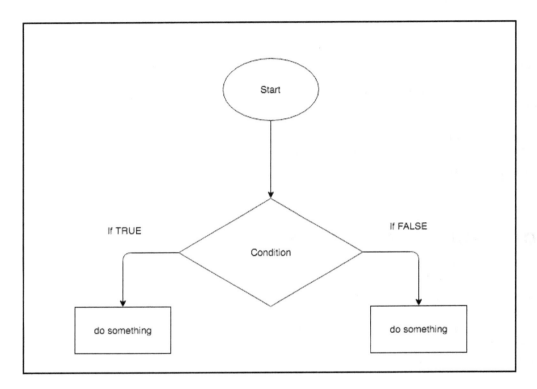

Conditional logic in code form might look something like the following (Python code):

```
# Python Conditional Logic Example
x = 0
if x == 0:
    print "Hello X is 0"
else:
    print "Hello X is NOT 0"
```

This Python code presents a simplistic example of conditional logic. It simply says that if x is equal to 0, then execute the `print` statement telling the user so. Within Jinja, we can implement a very similar set of logical operators. The only real difference in context is that within Jinja, all control structures and conditionalizations are wrapped within {% %} tags. Let's look at the same implementation using Jinja:

```
{% if condition %}
    execute_this
{% elif condition2 %}
    execute_this
{% else %}
    execute_this
{% endif %}
```

As we can see, the Jinja implementation also gives us the optional `else-if` statement. This provides us with additional capabilities when it comes to implementing conditional logic.

In Ansible, Jinja's conditional logic can be used in many different ways. It can be used to wrap entire tasks with a conditional statement (only execute these tasks if a variable is set). This provides a huge amount of flexibility and power to playbook developers. Let's look at a real-world example of implementing conditional logic within an Ansible playbook:

```
# Conditional Logic Playbook Example
---
- name: Hello World Conditional Logic
  user: root
  hosts: all
  vars:
    hello: true
    say_something: "{% if hello == true %} Hello Jinja {% else %} Goodbye
Ansible {% endif %}
  tasks:
    - debug:
        msg: "{{ say_something }}"
```

When we run this playbook, we get the following output:

```
root@ubuntu:/opt# ansible-playbook -i "localhost," -c local simpleplaybook.yml

PLAY [Hello World Playbook] ********************************************************

TASK [setup] **********************************************************************
ok: [localhost]

TASK [debug] **********************************************************************
ok: [localhost] => {
    "msg": " Hello "
}

PLAY RECAP ************************************************************************
localhost                  : ok=2    changed=0    unreachable=0    failed=0

root@ubuntu:/opt#
```

Based on the conditional statements we defined within our playbook:

```
hello: true
say_something: "{% if hello == true %} Hello Jinja {% else %} Goodbye
Ansible {% endif %}
```

We can flip the `hello` variable to false and get the following output:

```
root@ubuntu:/opt# ansible-playbook -i "localhost," -c local simpleplaybook.yml

PLAY [Hello World Playbook] ********************************************************

TASK [setup] **********************************************************************
ok: [localhost]

TASK [debug] **********************************************************************
ok: [localhost] => {
    "msg": " GoodBye "
}

PLAY RECAP ************************************************************************
localhost                  : ok=2    changed=0    unreachable=0    failed=0

root@ubuntu:/opt# _
```

It is important to note that Jinja syntax leveraged within an Ansible playbook will need to be inside of quotes and continue to adhere to YAML dictionary formatting standards. Jinja conditional syntax outside of the playbook (inside a Jinja template file) doesn't need to adhere to YAML standards.

Conditional logic can be compounded to provide significantly more flexibility and power within Ansible playbooks. In the example we saw, the `{% ... %}` tags were placed within the vars section, but they don't necessarily need to be there.

Aside from placing conditionals within an Ansible playbook directly, we can leverage Jinja conditional logic within a Jinja template file. This is where Jinja's true power can be felt. Let's look at an example of a Jinja template file implemented with conditional logic:

- Ansible playbook:

```
# Example Ansible playbook & Jinja Template
---
- name: Hello World Conditional Logic within a Jinja template
  user: root
  hosts: all
  vars:
    vhost:
        servername: my.server
        documentroot: /var/www
        serveradmin: bob
  tasks:

    # Jinja template file example
    - template:
        src: /jinjatemplates/httpdconf.j2
        dest: /etc/httpd/httpd.conf
        owner: root
        group: wheel
        mode: "u=rw,g=r,o=r"
```

- `httpdconf.j2`:

```
NameVirtualHost *:80

<VirtualHost *:80>
  ServerName {{ vhost.servername }}
  DocumentRoot {{ vhost.documentroot }}
{% if vhost.serveradmin is defined %}
  ServerAdmin {{ vhost.serveradmin }}
{% endif %}
  <Directory "{{ vhost.documentroot }}">
```

```
        AllowOverride All
        Options -Indexes FollowSymLinks
        Order allow,deny
        Allow from all
    </Directory>
</VirtualHost>
```

On running this example, Anisble will translate the Jinja template, transfer it over to the remote host, and place it in the `/etc/httpd/httpd.conf` directory.

Loops and iterators

No programming language would be complete without the capability of reducing the amount of code implemented by iterating over repetitive tasks, and Jinja is no exception. Jinja offers multiple loop types within its syntax arsenal. Loops can come in many forms within a modern traditional programming language. For example, most modern programming languages support most of the following loop types:

- `For` loops
- `Foreach` loops
- `While` loops
- `Do...Until` loops

In addition to these loop options, some programming languages support other OOP-oriented loop types. Within Ansible's implementation of Jinja, there is currently only support for the for loop. While the implementation of the types of loops is limited, there is the ability to perform counter-based iterations, list iterations, and compound loop conditionals. In this section, we will discuss loops within Jinja and learn how to implement them within our playbooks and our Jinja templates.

Simple counters

Counter loops involve the repetitive increment or decrement of a variable until a condition is met. Counter loops can be really useful for code that would only need a minor integer change as part of its iteration loop sequence. To better understand the concept of a counter loop, let's look at a flowchart illustration of a common programming loop that increments a counter:

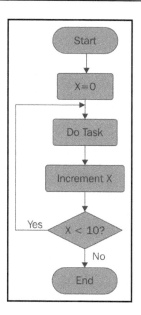

In this illustration, we basically repeat the increment task until the variable X is equal to the number 10. Once the evaluation of X is equal to 10, the iterator stops. The illustrated example of our loop could be represented in basic Python programming via the following syntax:

```
# Simple Python Counter Loop

x = 0
while x < 10:
    x+=1
print "The value of X is now" + str(x)
```

 Loops don't always need to perform mathematical operations. They can also execute automation, iterate over a list, or do pretty much anything your imagination can dream up. This example of a loop simply increments a counter.

Now that we have understood the basic concept of a loop, let's look at how we might implement the same type of loop within the context of Jinja and Ansible:

```
# Example Ansible playbook using an iterating loop
---
- name: Hello World Iterator within Ansible
  user: root
  hosts: all
```

```
tasks:
  - debug:
      msg: "{% for x in range (0,10) %} {{x}} {% endfor %}"
```

Simple enough implementation, right? The next obvious question is *how would we go about implementing this same type of logic within a Jinja template file*? I'm glad you asked! Let's take a look:

```
{% for id in range(201,221) %}
192.168.0.{{ id }} client{{ "%02d"|format(id-200) }}.vpn
{% endfor %}
```

Simple enough also, right? Beyond counting values within a loop, we can also iterate other data items.

List iterators

List iterators in programming solutions offer the ability to take a list of items and perform a sequence of operations on them. For example, we might have a list of fruit, [apples, oranges, grapes, pears], and want to iterate over this list. In traditional programming languages, we could use a foreach loop. The basic flow of a foreach loop might look something like the following:

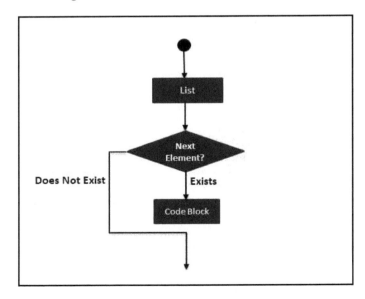

This example simply iterates through each item in the list and executes a code block based on the new list item presented. This type of implementation of looping is very basic within most programming languages, and Jinja is no exception. Based on this flow, we can look at a Python example and map this to the following code fragment:

```
# Simple example of a Python iterative loop

fruits = ['apples', 'oranges', 'pears', 'apricots']
# Iterate through a list of fruits
for fruit in fruits:
    print "A fruit of type: %s" % fruit
```

In Jinja, the implementation of the list iterator has the following syntax:

```
{# Example Jinja For iterator loop #}

{% for <item_name> in <list_name> %}
  code block
{% endfor %}
```

Finally, let's look at the translation of this loop sequence into Jinja:

- Hosts file:

```
[webservers]
webhost1.local
webhost2.local

[databaseservers]
dbserver1.local
dbserver2.local
```

- Playbook:

```
# Example of loops using Jinja
--
- name: Simple Ansible Playbook that loops over hosts within
Jinja
  vars:
    servers_to_configure: "{{ groups['databaseservers'] }}"
  tasks:
    - template:
      src: configfile.j2
      dest: configfile.conf
```

- Jinja template:

```
# Simple Configuration file based on Jinja templating

all_hosts += [
{% for host in servers_to_configure %}
  "{{ hostvars[host].ansible_default_ipv6.address }}"
{% endfor %}
]
```

Thise example will autopopulate a file titled `configfile.conf` and upload it to the target hosts with the contents transformed using the Jinja `for` iterator.

Complex iterators using Jinja

The iterators that we discussed earlier in this chapter are very simple in nature. Jinja also provides a more complex way of operating loops within Jinja. Complex (or compound) iterators are common practice within programming and are what make modern algorithms possible. A complex iterator may take many forms, but often includes adding additional compound conditionals or nested loops within the loop sequence. Let's look at a flowchart illustrating a complex iterator (nested loop):

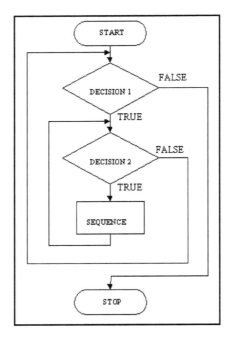

Does this flowchart looks pretty complex? It doesn't need to be. Let's look at the same algorithm in Python:

```
# Nested For Loop with Python

for iterating_var in sequence:
    for iterating_var in sequence:
        statements(s)
    statements(s)
```

In Jinja, implementing nested for loops can be done in much the same way. Let's look at an example:

```
# Example YAML variable file
var_name:
- group:
    - variable1
    - variable2
- group:
    - variable1
    - variable2
```

The Jinja template would look like the following:

```
{% for var in var_name %}
<group>
{% for host in var.group %}
    <variable><host>{{ host }}</host></variable>
{% endfor %}
</group>
{% endfor %}
```

As we can see, the implementation of this Jinja loop is also pretty simple. Let's take a look at how to make a slightly more complex loop that uses both iterators and conditionals. Following are the code fragments for variables in loops from a `vars` file:

```
# Save this as vars.yml
---
places:
- name: USA
capital: Blue
- name: Great Britan
capital: Yellow
- name: Itally
capital: Blue
- name: Mexico
capital: Yellow
- name: Ireland
```

```
capital: Yellow
- name: Amsterdam
capital: Orange
```

 # Save this as playbook.yml

```
---
- name: How to use variables in Jinja2 Loops
  hosts: localhost
  connection: local
  vars_files:
    - vars.yml
  gather_facts: no
  tasks:
    - name: This task uses a j2 template which has a series of loops
      template: src=./ourloop.j2 dest=./output.txt
```

 # Save this as ourloop.j2

```
{% for country in places %}
 Currently people are visiting {{ country }}.
{% endfor %}
```

Now run it and check the output. Nice right?

Applying Jinja in Ansible Playbook's

Jinja can be applied to playbooks in a few specific ways. The most common implementation of Jinja is the use of filters and variables within playbook YAML files. This information must be placed within the quoted context of YAML key/value structures. The key/value structure of YAML *does* normally support non-quoted values, but within the context of Jinja, we *must* have it within quotes. For example, let's consider the following:

```
---
- name: Simple Ansible Playbook that loops over hosts within Jinja
  vars:
    say_hello
    say_something: "{{ say_hello }}"

  tasks:
    - debug:
        msg: "{{ say_something }}"
```

As we can see from this playbook, the implementation of Jinja within the playbook has the {{...}} tags directly within quotes. The *only* location that supports non-quoted implementations of Jinja tags is within a Jinja template. Jinja templates are parsed differently from YAML and therefore support loose implementations of Jinja tags. Let's consider the following:

```
# Simple Configuration file based on Jinja templating

{% for host in servers_to_configure %}
  {{ host }}
{% endfor %}
```

Summary

In this chapter, we covered how Jinja specifically and uniquely fits within the Ansible world. We learned how Jinja filters work and discovered how these filters can be leveraged within a playbook to provide us with clever playbook implementations. In addition to Jinja filters, we spent time learning how to perform mathematical operations on variables within a Jinja filter context.

In addition to the concept of Jinja filters, we also learned about loops and iterators. These iterators provided us with good insights into iterating over structured data, counting forward and in reverse. We learned also that iterators can be used for iterating through lists (such as the list of fruits that we iterated over in our example). Finally, we learned how to apply Jinja within our playbooks and the specific requirements that surround leveraging Jinja.

In the next chapter, we will cover the Ansible vault. The Ansible vault represents a unique and secure solution for encrypting, storing, and decrypting data with Ansible. This solution is *highly* useful as it can be used to store password data, usernames, secure database queries, and so much more. Oftentimes within an organization, sensitive user data is needed to configure and deploy software. This sensitive data is often usernames and passwords. Ansible provides an out-of-the-box solution to help encrypt and hide sensitive information. The next chapter will be on the Ansible vault. The next chapter of the book will outline the Ansible way of managing, storing, and deploying sensitive information. We will cover how to best leverage the Ansible vault utility to ensure that sensitive data is kept safe and secret. We will learn (by example) how to best control and manage highly secure information and learn the underpinnings of how Ansible keeps your information secure.

Let's proceed to learning about the Ansible vault.

7
Ansible Vault

Modern day encryption solutions have come a long way since the initial concepts of encryption were invented and implemented back in the early days of computer science. Encryption and security are both hotbed topics within modern mainstream news outlets, as notable security breaches have initiated a heightened awareness of security fallacies and there has been an increase in guarding of sensitive data. With applications and customer's sensitive data moving toward the cloud, the necessity for an increased level of control and security is now greater than ever.

Modern **Infrastructure as Code (IaC)** solutions have paved the way for configuration management solutions to be stored within modern source control solutions. Managing and tracking infrastructure changes via a source control solution is highly valuable as it provides the ability for teams to ensure that IaC solutions are tracked through version control, and revisions are notated and backed up. In addition to these value points storing Ansible playbook's and related automation version control ensures teams can collaborate to create useful automation, Configuration Management solutions, and deployment tasks.

Creating playbook's and storing them within a modern source control solution makes a lot of sense and is a best practice. What does not make a lot of sense is storing sensitive data within source control. This is because it allows ANYONE with access to the source control solution to pry into potentially confidential information. Enter Ansible vault. It promises the ability to hide such sensitive data, to encrypt what is meant to be encrypted, and continues to allow playbook developers to store their playbooks in source control. Awesome right?

In this chapter, we will discover the Ansible vault. It provides us with a secure, easy-to-use solution to encrypt and store sensitive data within our playbook's or in a variables vault file. Specifically, in this chapter, we will cover the following subjects:

- The Ansible vault architecture
- Basic vault usage

- How data can be encrypted with Ansible vault
- How to create, edit, and encrypt variable files
- How to decrypt files in a secure manner
- How to embed encrypted data within a YAML playbook
- Running a playbook and decrypting data on the fly
- Tips and tricks to best use Ansible vault

Let's get started!

The Ansible Vault Architecture

Ansible vault is designed for playbook developers, system administrators, and related personnel to store sensitive data within a playbook, variable file, or directory structure. The encryption system employed by Ansible vault is based on the **Symmetrical Key Advanced Encryption System** or **AES Symmetrical Key** solution. The AES Symmetrical Key encryption provides us with an easy-to-use way of using the same key to encrypt data as well as decrypt data. The following diagram provides an illustration of **AES Symmetrical Key Encryption**:

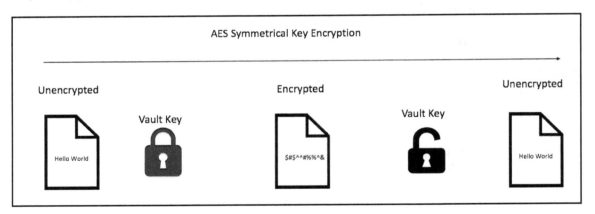

The Ansible vault solution has been designed to provide encryption services for any structured data file supported by Ansible. This means we can encrypt `group_vars/`, AND `host_vars/..` inventory variable directories. It also means we can encrypt variable files loaded within the `include_vars/vars_files`. As we can see from the preceding, the supported supported by Ansible's vault solution is vast. Basically in the end it means we can encrypt ANY and ALL data we want using the vault EXCEPT playbook's themselves.

Version 2.3 of Ansible includes a feature that supports encrypting single variable values within an Ansible YAML file. This is accomplished using the `!vault` tag. The result of this special tag allows us to inform Ansible to decrypt the value when processing the facts of the file.

In addition to the ability to encrypt variables and variable files, the entire playbook can be encrypted. More so, Ansible also supports the encryption of binary files, data files, and much more. These files can then be decrypted on the fly using `copy_file`. In addition to the copy file option, there are many others that are supported by Ansible vault. In the next sections, we will look at some examples of how to encrypt, decrypt, and rekey vault files on the fly and how we can leverage Ansible's vault later in the chapter. Before we dig into that, let's take a look at how to use the basic implementation of the Ansible vault and how to encrypt, decrypt, and rekey vault files.

Basic Vault Usage

Ansible vault's most basic implementation is a simple AES Symmetric Key encryption solution (as we discussed earlier). The implementation of this is managed through the command-line interface, specifically the `ansible-vault` command. Using this command, we have the ability to encrypt, decrypt, rekey, and edit vault specific files. The syntax of each of these commands along with a description and example is provided next.

Encrypting an Ansible vault YAML file

This command syntax allows us to encrypt the contents of a YAML file. Upon executing, it will prompt the user for the key they wish to use in order to encrypt it.

The content of the `my_vault.yml` file is shown here:

```
integer: 25
string: "Hello Ansible Users"
float: 25.0
boolean: Yes
```

Then, in order to encrypt the file, execute the following command:

```
#> ansible-vault encrypt my_vault.yml
```

The output of the command execution is shown next:

```
New Vault password:
Confirm New Vault password:
#>
```

Once the file is encrypted, we can see the encryption via the `cat` command, as shown next:

```
root@ubuntu:/opt/chp7# cat vault.yml
$ANSIBLE_VAULT;1.1;AES256
34623461333032363361393534353132643935376463323731376363356664353464303632643139
37633663313430643839373961333066353233362643163360a3930373964326235336239393353239
38653834333032643538616130646264383731323562366637623537333461333565303834363136
37393134653436376406a66333396537363435646534376232303235326293265343461636431303038
64366238303265534663235313965546636396534633032303533335386331616533373832613030066
61396463363262666353562633130623332353337323533664343662633323316639383437363933661
3834663732386338376536343661376637665
root@ubuntu:/opt/chp7#
```

This example shows a simple way to encrypt and decrypt data using Ansible vault. This tactic is useful from a command line and manual input perspective, but it adds a human element to our automation execution that we may not always want. Encrypting files can also be done via a single command-line entry, as shown here:

```
$> ansible-vault encrypt my_vault.yml --vault-password-file vault_pass.txt
Encryption successful
```

In this example, we can see that Ansible vault has the option of taking in a password file. The `vault_pass.txt` is simply a flat text file that contains the Ansible vault password. This command-line instructs Ansible to use the password in the text file instead of prompting for a password. This option makes automating the vault a lot easier as there is no required human intervention.

To decrypt

The `decrypt` option of Ansible vault decrypts the contents of a previously encrypted YAML vault file. Upon executing it, Ansible vault will prompt the user for the vault password to decrypt the file. Once the password has been inputted, Ansible uses AES Symmetric Key encryption to decrypt the file (if the correct key was entered). Let's look at an example.

First, let's start with our encrypted file that we created in the previous section on encrypting using Ansible vault. A screenshot of the encrypted vault file is provided next:

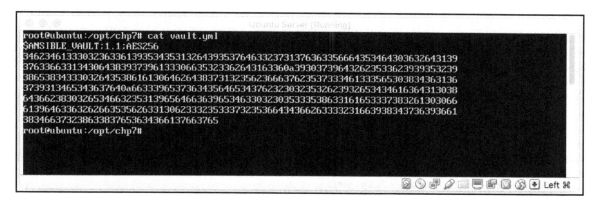

Then, decrypt the file using the following command:

```
#> ansible-vault decrypt my_vault.yml
```

The output of the execution of this command would be the following:

```
#> Vault password:
Decryption successful
```

Once the file is decrypted, we can see the decrypted file as such:

Similar to the encryption mechanism we talked about earlier, we can also specify the vault key in the keyfile form on the command line. This will help us better automate things and remove the need for us to manually type the password. An example is shown next:

```
$> ansible-vault decrypt my_vault.yml --vault-password-file vault_pass.txt
Encryption successful
```

To rekey an Ansible vault file

Changing the key that Ansible vault uses to encrypt/decrypt a vault file is a fairly simplistic task. It simply involves using the `rekey` operator within the Ansible vault command-line context. In the following example, the `rekey` command syntax is shown:

```
#> ansible-vault rekey <file.yml>
```

Upon running the previous command, we will be prompted for the existing key and a new key. The output (if the `rekey` was a success) should look something like the following:

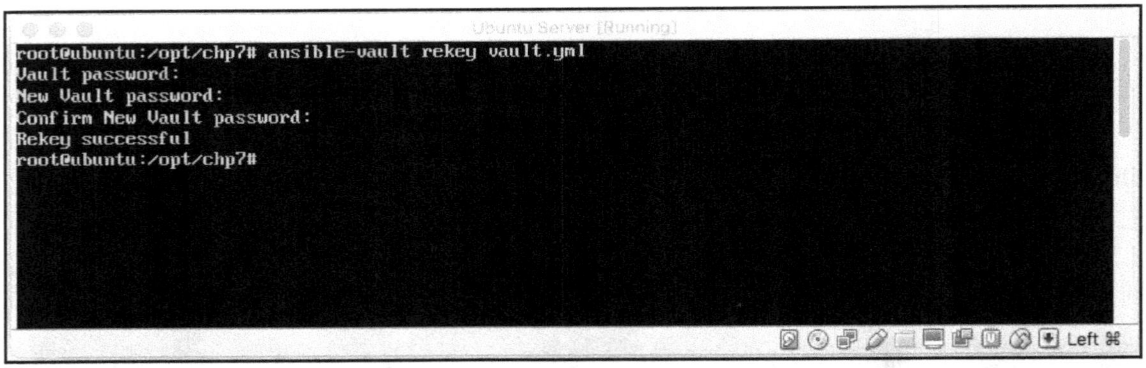

Editing in place

The Ansible vault solution provides a handy way of editing vault encrypted information on the fly using the default system editor. Within the context of a Linux operating system, the default editor can be set on the command line using the following command syntax:

```
export EDITOR='vi'
```

In the previous code, we set the editor to be `vi`; however, you can set it to any editor of your preference [`nano`, `pico`, `vi`, `vim`, and so on).

 Usually on Linux systems, the default editor is usually set to `vi`.

Now that we have the default editor in place, we can edit our Ansible vault data by issuing the `edit` command option in conjunction with the `ansible-vault` command. Let's look at an example:

```
#> ansible-vault edit my_vault.yml
```

Decrypting the vault when running a playbook

Encrypting, decrypting, and rekeying Ansible vault data manually is one thing; using this information on the fly within the context of playbook execution is what we really want to achieve. In this section, we will cover how to decrypt the Ansible vault encrypted data within the context of playbook execution.

There are two ways to automatically decrypt the vault data embedded within a playbook or variables file. The first is by storing the vault key within a flat text file and then passing this key file to the `ansible-playbook` command. The second is to use the `--ask-vault-pass` command-line option to prompt the user for the vault password. Let's take a look at how each of these options works.

Automatically decrypting using password files

The most desirable way to decrypt Ansible vaulted data is to do so without user intervention. This option opens the door for a more flexible automation approach (initiating it through Jenkins, CircleCI, Bamboo, or whatever). To implement this solution, the trick is to store the Ansible vault password within a password file. For example, if we were to have a `vars` file, we would encrypt it using the `encrypt` option and then store the key we used to encrypt it in the flat text file. Then, when running the `ansible-playbook` command, we could pass the `vault-password-file` directly. The syntax of this is shown next:

```
$> ansible-playbook -i inventory/qa.hosts playbooks/example.yml --vault-
password-file ~/.vault_pass.txt
```

The password should be a string stored as a single line in the file.

Manually decrypting vault data

The alternative approach to decrypting Ansible vaulted data would be to have Ansible prompt the user for the password upon executing the playbook. This can be accomplished in a simple manner as well. The following command syntax shows how to instruct Ansible to prompt the user for the vault password prior to executing a playbook:

```
$> ansible-playbook -i inventory/qa.hosts playbooks/example.yml --ask-
vault-pass
```

Real-world Ansible Vault Workflow

The Ansible vault implementation is a really robust solution designed to provide security for sensitive information. The implementation (as you learned already) allows us to encrypt, decrypt, rekey, and edit private data with ease. As easy as the vault is to use, finding a maintainable way to utilize the Ansible vault is not always easily apparent. As such, within this section, we will discuss some tips and tricks that can make your Ansible vault experience a bit more enjoyable.

Ansible vault with roles

The Ansible vault implementation is best leveraged in conjunction with roles. Roles (as we discussed earlier) allow us to modularize our playbooks and reuse functionality within them. The specific area of the roles implementation we are going to look at would be the vars folder. The vars folder is where we define our variables and data points that are then used by the tasks and plays.

To begin with this tutorial, let's start by creating an Ansible playbook with the following folder and file structure (the contents of the files can be blank for now, as we will fill in the details in just a moment):

```
root@ubuntu:/opt/chp7# tree
├── playbook.yml
└── roles
    └── vaulttest
        ├── tasks
        │   └── main.yml
        └── vars
            └── sensitive_data.yml

4 directories, 3 files
root@ubuntu:/opt/chp7#
```

Once created, there are a few things that should become immediately apparent. The first is that the playbook we are creating is a simple vault test with a single role and a `sensitive_data` variable's implementation. Also, as you may have guessed, we will be using the `sensitive_data.yml` file to store our super secret information. The contents of this file should reflect the following:

```
---
secret_text: |
  The contents of this message are secret. This tape will explode in 5
seconds.
```

As we can see from the provided file content, we have a simple vars file with a variable defined within, titled `secret_text`.

The YAML syntax supports multi-line variable implementations. This is accomplished via the | or pipe character, which is provided at the end of the line.

Now that sensitive data has been created, let's encrypt our vars file using the Ansible vault encrypt command. This is accomplished via the following command-line entry:

```
#> ansible-vauult encrypt sensitive_data.yml
```

Now that the file is encrypted, we can create our role file, call it the `main.yml` file, and populate our role information. The contents of `main.yml` should look like the following:

```
---
- include_vars: sensitive_data.yml
- name: Copy sensitive data file from Ansible control server to target
hosts
  copy:
    content="{{secret_text}}"
    dest=/tmp/secret_text.txt
```

Finally, let's create our `playbook.yml` file. These files are going to be really simple and only point to a single role (`vaulttest`). Let's take a look at the contents of these files:

```
---
# File: playbook.yml
- hosts: all

roles:
 - { role: vaulttest }
```

Now that we have all our files created, let's go ahead and `commit` our code to source control (if applicable) and test it out. The command to run the solution is provided next:

```
#> ansible-playbook -i 'localhost,' -c local playbook.yml --ask-vault-pass
```

The following is the output you should see when running it:

```
Ubuntu Server [Running]
root@ubuntu:/opt/chp7# ansible-playbook -i 'localhost,' -c local playbook.yml --ask-vault-pass
Vault password:

PLAY ***********************************************************************

TASK [setup] ***************************************************************
ok: [localhost]

TASK [vaulttest : include_vars] ********************************************
ok: [localhost]

TASK [vaulttest : Copy sensitive data] *************************************
ok: [localhost]

PLAY RECAP *****************************************************************
localhost                  : ok=3    changed=0    unreachable=0    failed=0
```

Summary

In this chapter, you learned about Ansible vault. You also learned how to encrypt files, decrypt them, rekey an encrypted file, edit them on the fly, and use the data within a playbook. Ansible vault provides us with a really simple way to encrypt and store encrypted data. As we saw through examples, the encrypting and decrypting of files within the ansible vault architecture does not need to be complex or complicated. The techniques we discussed within this chapter have wide applicable use within an IT operations- or DevOps-oriented organization.

In the next chapter, we will talk about Ansible's wide arrange of module and libraries. This chapter will help us identify some of the more popular modules and libraries that Ansible provides to integrate it with other tools. Let's proceed.

8
Ansible Modules and Libraries

Ansible provides integration and compatibility for hundreds of open and closed source software solutions. This integration opens the door for Ansible to communicate at a programmatic API level with a multitude of build, test, project management, cloud, and delivery software solutions. The module implementation, as a result, provides Ansible with a huge edge against competing automation and configuration management solutions on the market.

At this point in the book, we should be fairly well educated about some of the more common playbook implementations and structured approaches to leverage Ansible. To expand our knowledge further, this chapter will focus on the wide array of modules provided by the Ansible core implementation. Modules in Ansible provide the ability for playbooks to connect to and control third-party technologies (some open source, some closed source). In this chapter, we will discuss the most popular ones and dive into creating playbook tasks that help manage a suite of tools and services available to developers, testers, and operators.

To further our learning, in this chapter, we will take a look at the integration that Ansible provides with other software solutions. As we take a journey through this chapter, and will learn about some of the more popular integration points available within the Ansible realm. We will discover how Ansible's modular architecture works and learn how it provides hooks for integration with other technologies.

The topics we will specifically cover in this chapter include the following:

- Introducing Ansible modules
- Integrating Ansible with other technologies

- Understanding the integration options available within the Ansible documentation for various technologies
- Step-by-step examples of integrating Ansible with other technologies

Let's get started!

Introducing Ansible Modules

Ansible modules represent the preferred way of connecting Ansible (and automating) with other software solutions. At the time of writing of this book, Ansible has the ability to integrate with a multitude of external software and hardware solutions. Some of the more obvious integrations we have already discovered include the following:

- Linux (OS and packages)
- Filesystem management
- Package management

These basic modules that we have discussed so far are obvious for introductory playbook creation and management, but did you know that Ansible integrates with JIRA, Slack, Git, Artifactory, Jenkins, and *much much* more. Ansible module's exhaustive integration has been broken down within the Ansible documentation into the following categories:

- Cloud modules
- Clustering modules
- Commands modules
- Crypto modules
- Database modules
- Files modules
- Identity modules
- Inventory modules
- Messaging modules
- Monitoring modules
- Net tools modules
- Network modules
- Notification modules
- Packaging modules

- Remote management modules
- Source control modules
- Storage modules
- System modules
- Utilities modules
- Web infrastructure modules
- Windows modules

As you can see from the preceding list, Ansible provides a vast expanse of integrations with other technologies. Each integration point with another technology is leveraged via an Ansible playbook task. The complete documentation of each integration module can be found at http://docs.ansible.com/ansible/modules_by_category.html.

Ansible divides the module implementation into a few distinct categories: the Core, Community, Curated module set, and Custom modules, and plugins. Each is implemented in a very similar way but is organized by Ansible slightly differently. The diagram provided next shows where the Ansible module implementation sits within the Ansible architecture:

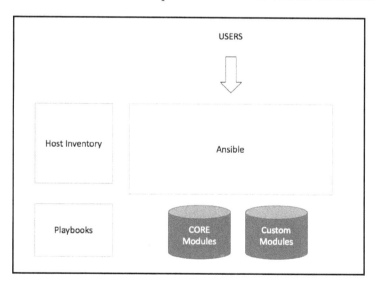

In the previous chapters of this book, we have been using Ansible modules for basic system-level configurations, package management, file operations, and more. These implementations have taught us how to make use of the core Ansible module set.

The Ansible implementation has three different module types. These module types are Core, Curated, Community, and Custom. Each of these modules have their own specific function and role within the Ansible solution. Let's take a minute to look at what the Ansible documentation has to say about these different module types:

- **Core**: These are modules that the core ansible team maintains and will always ship with ansible itself. They will also receive slightly higher priority for all requests. Non-core modules are still fully usable.
- **Curated**: Some examples of Curated modules are submitted by other companies or maintained by the community. Maintainers of these types of modules must watch for any issues reported or pull requests raised against the module.

Core Committers will review all modules becoming Curated. Core Committers will review proposed changes to existing Curated modules once the community maintainers of the module have approved the changes. Core committers will also ensure that any issues that arise due to Ansible engine changes will be remediated. Also, it is strongly recommended (but not presently required) for these types of modules to have unit tests.

These modules are currently shipped with Ansible, but might be shipped separately in the future.

- **Community**: These modules are not supported by Core Committers or by companies/partners associated to the module. They are maintained by the community.

They are still fully usable, but the response rate to issues is purely up to the community. Best effort support will be provided but is not covered under any support contracts.

These modules are currently shipped with Ansible, but will most likely be shipped separately in the future.

In the Ansible world, Ansible modules are also referred to as **task-plugins** or **library-plugins**, thus describing the way Ansible handles module implementations. Each module (Core or otherwise) is manifested via the pluggable architecture that is Ansible.

Within the context of an Ansible, modules offer a similar functionality to programming libraries. These libraries can be invoked via a playbook task *or* a direct single command-line operation. Let's take a quick look at each of these two implementation options.

Let's call an Ansible module from the command line:

```
ansible webservers -m service -a "name=httpd state=started"
ansible webservers -m ping
ansible webservers -m command -a "/sbin/reboot -t now"
```

Let's call an Ansible module from a playbook task:

```
- name: reboot the servers
  action: command /sbin/reboot -t now
```

From the preceding examples, we can see two distinct implementations of Ansible modules. Now that we can see how Ansible modules are executed (for system calls), let's take a look at how Ansible modules can provide connectivity solutions for other technologies.

Integrating Ansible with Other Technologies

Ansible integrates quite nicely with other technologies. The implementation of the module system provides us with a set of unique hooks that we can leverage to connect Ansible (on an API level) with popular software solutions. In this section of implementing Ansible with DevOps, we will take a closer look at how to actually use Ansible to connect with some of the more popular technology solutions available to DevOps-minded individuals.

Ansible with JIRA

Ansible provides us with a handy set of built-in tasks that can be used to *create* tickets. For those of you unfamiliar with JIRA, it is a widely used ticketing system created and maintained by Atlassian (http://www.atlassian.com). In this section, we will take a look at how to create and manipulate JIRA tickets using Ansible. The general implementation uses the JIRA module provided by Ansible. The following is an example of how to create a ticket using an Ansible task:

```
# Create a new JIRA ticket and add a comment to it:
- name: Create an issue
  jira:
  uri: "http://pathtojira"
  username: '{{ user }}'
  password: '{{ pass }}'
  project: ANSIBLE
  operation: create
  summary: Hello Ansible Jira Integration
  description: Created using Ansible JIRA module
  issuetype: Task
```

```
register: issue
```

Note that the preceding implementation uses Jinja to supply the module with a JIRA username and password. This might be best implemented using Ansible vault (which we just discovered in the previous chapter).

Beyond simple ticket creation, Ansible can also be used to modify existing tickets. Let's take a look at an example of that next:

```
# Transition an issue in JIRA by changing its status to done
- name: Mark the issue as resolved
  jira:
  uri: "http://pathtojira"
  username: '{{ user }}'
  password: '{{ pass }}'
  issue: '{{ issue.meta.key }}'
  operation: transition
  status: Resolved
```

For a complete documentation set of how to manipulate Jira tickets using Ansible, visit `http ://docs.ansible.com/ansible/jira_module.html#synopsis`.

Ansible and Git

Ansible provides a complete module to manipulate Git repositories. For those unfamiliar with Git, Git is a modern distributed source control solution currently in use by a significant number of software organizations. Unlike traditional server/client-oriented source control solutions, Git provides a nifty distributed solution, which does not require a central server. Ansible's integration with Git is fairly robust. It provides a complete set of integration tasks. The complete documentation for the Ansible Git module can be found at `http://docs.ans ible.com/ansible/git_module.html`.

Let's take a look at some example playbook tasks and see how we can integrate Ansible and Git.

 One prerequisite for Ansible's Git integration is that the target machine should have Git v1.7 or a higher command-line client installed and working.

Here's an example Git checkout task:

```
# An Ansible task example which checks out source code
- git:
  repo: 'https://mygitserver.com/the/path/to/repo.git'
  dest: /opt/sourcecode
  version: release-0.23
```

Here's an example where we'll be creating ZIP file from the GitHub repository:

```
# Example of how to create a ZIP from a GitHub repository
- git:
    repo: https://github.com/foo/implementingdevops-examples.git
    dest: /src/implementingdevops-examples
    archive: /tmp/examples.zip
```

Ansible and Jenkins

Jenkins CI (Open sourced by CloudBees) is a modern day Continuous Integration and Continuous Delivery solution. It is widely leveraged by organizations of all sizes and supports simple automation as well as complex build and delivery pipeline implementations. It has a massive

Ansible integrates with Jenkins in a few different ways. For the purpose of this chapter, the one we will talk about is the module-specific integration point. That is, we will be automating the control of Jenkins itself using Ansible. In this section, you will learn about some interesting ways in which you can use Ansible to control and manage the Jenkins instance via Ansible. The complete documentation for the Ansible Jenkins module can be found at `http://docs.ansible.com/ansible/jenkins_job_module.html`.

Ansible communicates with Jenkins over the Jenkins REST API. So it is important that the Jenkins instance have the REST API available and can be reached from the target server that will be connecting to the REST API. In addition to the REST API availability, the Ansible Jenkins module requires the following Python packages to be installed:

- Python-Jenkins 0.4.12 or higher
- lxml 3.3.3 or higher

These packages are required because they provide direct API connectivity to Jenkins from Python. This is something Ansible has no direct connection to and as such they are required to use this specific module.

Now that we have the prerequisites taken care of, let's look at some examples of Ansible tasks:

```
# Jenkins REST API to create a jenkins job
- jenkins_job:
  config: "{{ lookup('file', 'templates/test.xml') }}"
  name: test
  password: admin
  url: http://localhost:8080
  user: admin
```

In addition to creating jobs based on templates, we can also delete jobs. The following example shows how to do that:

```
# Delete a jenkins job using the Ansible Jenkins module
- jenkins_job:
    name: foo
    password: my_admin
    state: absent
    url: http://pathtojenkinsurl:8080
    user: admin
```

For a complete Jenkins REST API documentation, check out the following URL:

`https://www.cloudbees.com/blog/taming-jenkins-json-api-depth-and-tree`

Ansible and Docker

Docker has become a powerhouse in the virtualization space within the last few years. Docker has a unique kernel, filesystem, and memory management solution, which makes Docker an ideal choice in virtualization for many organizations. Docker operates under the concept of container-based visualizations, which are lightweight virtualized operating systems. In this section, we will look at how Ansible integrates with Docker. We will discover how to control Docker containers using Ansible 2. The complete Ansible Docker module reference can be found at `http://docs.ansible.com/ansible/docker_module.html`.

In order to make use of the Docker Ansible module, the following Python packages must be installed on the target system (the system running the playbook):

- Python 2.6 or higher
- Docker-py 0.3.0 or higher
- Docker server 0.10.0 or higher

Ansible provides a number of docker-oriented modules, which provides interconnectivity with Ansible and Docker. The complete list and descriptions of each is provided as follows (`https://docs.ansible.com/ansible/guide_docker.html`):

- `docker_service`: Use your existing Docker compose files to orchestrate containers on a single Docker daemon or on Swarm. Supports compose versions 1 and 2
- `docker_container`: Manages the container life cycle by providing the ability to create, update, stop, start, and destroy a container
- `docker_image`: Provides full control over images, including `build`, `pull`, `push`, `tag`, and `remove`
- `docker_image_facts`: Inspects one or more images in the Docker host's image cache, providing the information as facts to make decision or assertions in a playbook
- `docker_login`: Authenticates with Docker Hub or any Docker registry and updates the Docker Engine config file, which in turn provides password-free pushing and pulling of images to and from the registry
- `docker (dynamic inventory)`: Dynamically builds an inventory of all the available containers from a set of one or more Docker hosts

It's important to note that the `docker_container` task name has been deprecated in Ansible 2.2. Instead, Ansible recommends that you use `docker_container` and `docker_image` instead.

Let's look at some simple playbook task examples that will integrate Ansible with Docker.

This is how we can use Ansible to build a Docker container:

```
# How to build a docker image using Ansible
- name: Build a docker image
  docker_image: >
  name=docker-image-created-by-ansible
  tag=ansibleexample1
  path=/tmp/site
  state=present
```

This is how you can use the command line to build a Docker container:

```
- name: How to build an image with the command line
  command: docker build -t build-container-using-ansible-command:ex2
/tmp/site
```

This is a complete example:

```
---
- name: Build a docker container using the command line
  hosts: all

tasks:
  - name: build a docker container
    command: docker build -t build-a-docker-container:ex2b ./site

- name: run a site within a docker container
  docker:
    name: mysite
    image: "build-a-docker-container:ex2b"
    state: reloaded
    publish_all_ports: yes
    use_tls: encrypt
```

Summary

In this chapter, we looked at the Ansible module architecture. We talked about how Ansible organizes modules by category (Core and user). Once you learned how Ansible manages modules, we talked about how Ansible modules can be called via two distinct methods (the command line and via playbook tasks). Then, we moved on and looked at a few examples of popular integration modules with Ansible.

In the next chapter, we will move on to look at how to integrate Ansible with popular CICD solutions, such as Jenkins, Git, and more. We will explore how to start making pipelines using Ansible and discover some tricks that will help us encourage the reuse of Ansible playbooks within an organization. Let's get moving, shall we?

Integrating Ansible with CI and CD Solutions

9

Ansible, DevOps, Agile, **Continuous Integration** (CI), and **Continuous Delivery** (CD) implementations go hand in hand. Each transitions smoothly into the next. Through Ansible's comprehensive module implementation that we learned about in the last chapter, we can saw how Ansible integrates quite nicely with many industry standard Agile, Continuous Integration and Continuous Delivery solutions. Some of the more common CI->CD solutions that Ansible integrates with include Jenkins, Artifactory, Maven, Bamboo, and so on. Ansible integrates with these solutions so tightly that in fact, Ansible even has a complete CI->CD integration guide provided at the following URL `https://www.ansible.com/continuous-delivery`.

For those unfamiliar with Continuous Integration and Continuous Delivery, these solutions have taken the software development world by storm. They propose a modern standardized way for committing, building, delivering, and testing code via software automation. The progression of code to production through automation and process is called a pipeline. The result of implementing a CI->CD pipelines is a highly effective way of automating the release of a software project by creating a repeatable process, and providing the team members with automatic feedback loops on the quality.

CI->CD best practices aim to provide a highly reliable way to build and keep a software project releasable at any moment in time. This is accomplished through a combination of highly disciplined development practices and automation of the build, delivery, and testing apparatuses of the software solution. By combining some fundamental practices with automation, an organization can become highly efficient at developing and delivering code.

In this chapter, we will begin to look at Continuous Integration and Continuous Delivery. We will take a deep dive into the fundamental constructs associated with each and provide details on how to integrate Ansible with popular CI->CD solutions that are readily available. Specifically, in this chapter, we will cover the following topics:

- Overview of Continuous Integration
- Overview of Continuous Delivery
- Ansible's Role in a CI->CD oriented organization
- Integrating Ansible with Jenkins
- Integrating Ansible with Vagrant

Let's begin exploring this crucial integration piece.

Overview of Continuous Integration

Continuous integration, otherwise known as CI, has been around for quite some time. Its origins can be traced back to Kent Beck, Martin Fowler, and their work at the Chrysler corporation in the mid-nineties. The basic idea was that organizations could save a significant amount of time and effort by performing small yet frequent code merges into a central mainline within source control instead of a large risky merge just prior to release.

This way of thinking requires a team to discipline itself fairly well and requires that each team member commit their code frequently. It discourages isolated feature development efforts for long periods of time and encourages a higher level of collaboration and communication. The result of such an implementation is a much higher quality release due to less complex merge conflicts and code integration issues.

The idea of continuous integration has been a trending topic for years. This is because of the higher level of communication that is required for it to become a successful practice. Beyond the basic commit stage, CI also includes an automated verification system and notification feedback loop so stakeholders can be notified if the commit and merge were defective. This notification system provides instant feedback on the quality of the commit.

Software development professionals have debated the effectiveness of this solution for quite some time and will continue to debate in the future. Generally, the practice of CI can be described with the following diagram:

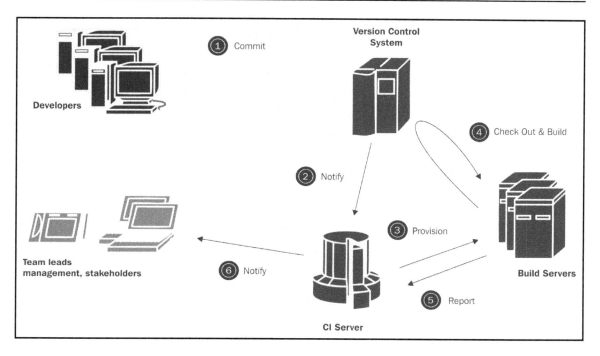

As we can see from this diagram, continuous integration spans the full development life cycle of a software project. This specifically includes the following stages:

- Code development collaboration
- Code commit and merging
- Automation-based provisioning of build/development environment
- Automation-based builds
- Automation-based testing of the completed builds (unit test, code coverage, lint and style tests)
- Automation based packaging of the build results (binaries and deliverables)

Continuous integration concepts and practices

As we mentioned earlier, the concept of Continuous Integration is not new. The general practice of implementing a continuous integration oriented development team requires a change in mindset across the team, a level of engineering collaboration applied across the team, and a set of basic required practices. These practices are outlined in the list here:

- Mainline development (no source-control-based branches or highly frequent branch merges).
- A CI based automation system that:
    - Automatically checks out code onto a system
    - Verifies the compilability of the source code
    - Notifies users of any failures

The branching concept of CI over a period of time would look something like what is shown in the following diagram:

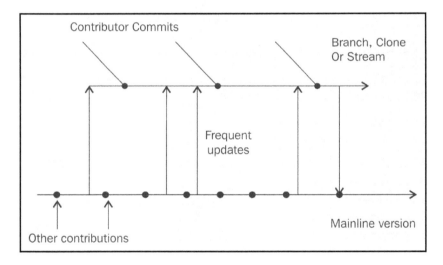

Based on this illustration, we can see that in a Continuous Integration environment, developers would be required to push and pull from a central mainline frequently. Each push is then automatically verified using an automated build and test system. Any failures are reported to the larger team and stakeholders.

If a failure is reported by the system, all commits and pushes to the system should stop until the error is fixed. This is because the system is *not* in a known working state and that failed state must be fixed in order to prevent compounded errors.

 While CI generally encourages mainline development, it is possible to achieve Continuous Integration with branches. The main requirement of CI is to have developers remain in sync with the mainline. If a branching system is adopted, strict discipline will need to be maintained in order to ensure branch development does not go on in isolation for long periods of time.

The result of implementing a CI solution is commit phase elements within a build pipeline. Now that we have an understanding of what CI is and how it might work, let's look at Continuous Delivery.

Handling unfinished work

When working in a Continuous Integration or Continuous Delivery development environment, there is often a common misconception that developers need source control branching as a way to isolate unfinished work. This branch-based development is the antithesis of a Continuous Integration pattern. As such, there are structures and development practices that can be implemented to allow CI and CD to continue without the need for extraneous branches within source control. Let's spend a few minutes looking at the options available to developers who want to satisfy Continuous Integration without having their work complete.

Branch by abstraction

Branching by abstraction provides a solid way for developers to continue working on an incomplete implementation and they not need to create a new branch. The idea behind the branching by abstraction architecture is simple:

1. Modularize the architecture of the software system.
2. Replace dated modules by simply creating a new class or folder structure on side by side the old one.
3. Swap out the calls to the module.

The basic implementation documented earlier can also be summarized with the following diagram:

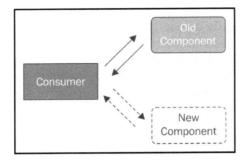

As we can see from the architecture, the new component is simply interchanged from the old one once it has been completed and deemed functional. This allows the source control level for the components to be committed and pushed without the need for a new branch.

Feature toggles

Feature toggles are another way to provide a comprehensive CI implementation. Feature toggles exist in the form of switches. Switches can be turned off/turned on via a configuration change, UI implementation switch, or other configurable objects.

Software programming languages provide the ability to feature toggle code by nature. The most simple example of a feature toggle would be a simple `if/else` condition, as shown here:

```
# Simple Feature toggle
if x in y:
  # Do something
```

Beyond a programmatic implementation, a feature toggle's basic flow of operation would be something like what is shown in the following figure:

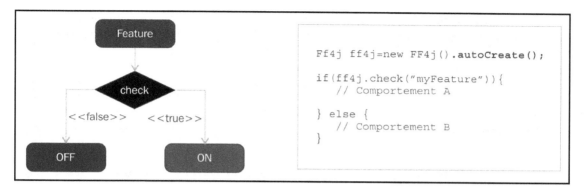

```
Ff4j ff4j=new FF4j().autoCreate();

if(ff4j.check("myFeature")){
    // Comportement A

} else {
    // Comportement B
}
```

Feature toggles allow us to commit code into the mainline and even push that code into production without the necessary overhead of creating a branch.

A/B testing patterns

A/B testing is a relatively new addition to the software landscape. For those not familiar with it, the user base is presented with two distinct data implementations. Depending on which implementation the user base likes best, the feature that is the most popular gets rolled out to the larger audience and becomes permanent. Let's look at a simple diagram of A/B testing:

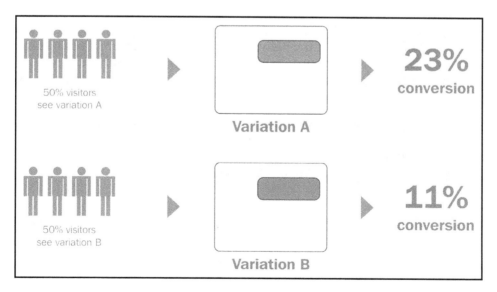

As we can see in the preceding diagram, A/B testing allows us to expose only a certain percentage of users to a feature and thus use that control group as a testing ground for whether the feature is useful. This type of implementation helps reduce the risk of over-engineering a feature only to find out it's not actually valuable.

Generally, A/B testing aims to save an organization time and money. These savings provide the business with better agility and higher competency in becoming/remaining competitive. Even though the diagram illustrates 50% of users being shown a **Variation B**, it does not always need to be an exact 50%.

For example, if we were doing A/B properly, we might show *only* 1% of users a feature and leave the other 99% on the stable version. Then, if the 1% generally approves of the feature, we might expand that scope.

At this point in time, you may be asking where and how Ansible fits into A/B testing. This would be a great question. Ansible provides us with a way of targeting hosts with our playbook's. As such, 1% of users may simply be delegated to a single host-oriented deployment. However, in most cases, you wouldn't want to just deploy an upgrade to a single host. Instead, you might consider something like blue-green deployments.

Overview of Continuous Delivery

Continuous Delivery was conceptualized by Jez Humble in 2012 with his revolutionary book on Continuous Delivery. The idea that Humble had when writing the book was to extend the concept of CI to support the delivery and automated testing apparatuses a software team would undertake prior to release. This concept radically changed the way software organizations looked at releasing software solutions to customers and aims to keep the software releasable at any time.

In the previous years of software development, having and maintaining a build system was considered a best practice. However, once the build was completed and unit tests all passed, there were still numerous manual processes that needed to be maintained in order to ensure the software solution was, in fact, releasable.

Some of the more popular post build tasks include the following:

- Installation verification
- Quality assurance testing
- Deployment environment provisioning
- Deployment
- Post-deployment verification

As software companies suffered more and more failures, those who were managing software projects realized that manually performing these tasks can become error-prone and time-consuming. These tasks also increased in complexity as the software systems they were building grew in size and increased in the user base. The solution Jez proposed was a repeatable and highly automated advance to Continuous Integration. He titled the implementation Continuous Delivery, or CD.

Continuous Delivery defined

CD, as we mentioned earlier, aimed to extend the implementation of CI. This way, a software system remains in a releasable state. This is accomplished by combining mainline development practices, Continuous Integration automation a set of automated provisioning and deployment solutions (to pre-production environments), and automated testing.

In a Continuous Delivery oriented organization, deployment pipelines are created to help implement the previously listed solutions. An example of a high-level deployment pipeline is shown next:

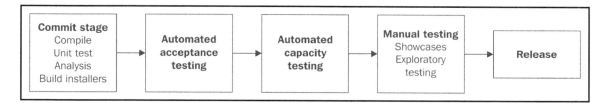

The deployment pipeline shown here is pretty simple in nature. It simply shows a commit flowing from a developer's hands into production and release. In the following diagram, we can see how a deployment pipeline looks from a bit lower of a view:

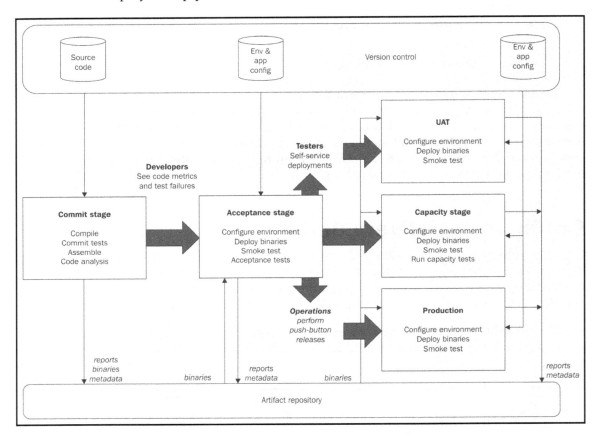

From the shown diagram, we can see that there are a few more visible components within the build pipeline. These components include the following:

- An artifact repository
- Version control
- Push button deployments
- Configuration management
- Smoke tests
- Functional tests

- Capacity tests
- A production stage

These additional components of Continuous Delivery are important. Let's go over each and see what they do or aim to accomplish:

- **Version control**: Version control aims to allow a central location for developers to communicate their code changes with the larger group. Some examples of modern version control systems include Git, Mercurial, SVN, and Perforce. The version control system allows not only easy communication but also the reverting of faulty code.
- **Artifact repository**: Adding a structured **Digital Media Library** (**DML**) to your organization is an important step in relation to implementing Continuous Delivery. This represents a definitive location where the output of the build system can be versioned and kept as a release approaches. It also allows multiple versions of the same.
- **Push button deployments**: Push button deployments are solutions that can be automatically deployed via a single button push.

This is how the solution can be deployed:

1. The automation pulls the binary from the artifact repository.
2. The automation pushes the artifact using a configuration management solution.
3. The artifact is unzipped and the automation inside is executed to perform the deployment.

Let's look at the other component in detail:

- **Configuration management**: In this step, a configuration management solution (such as Ansible) is used to deploy/configure the software installation onto the target environment machine.
- **Smoke tests**: Smoke tests are high-level functional tests that determine whether the software is worth testing further.
- **Functional tests**: Functional tests are verification tests (automated) that verify that the software meets business functional requirements. Each test suite within a functional test solution should be parallelized where possible in order to ensure that there is no bottleneck in performance when executing these tests.
- **Capacity tests/stress tests**: This type of test helps validate that the software can operate and perform effectively under normal traffic loads from the potential user base. Often, this type of test is overlooked, which results in unscalable software solutions that crash under heavy load.

Handling complex and long running builds and deployments

Sometimes, a build or deployment will be time-consuming (multiple different components or complicated environment setup steps). When this happens, Continuous Delivery-oriented organizations can handle this as well. This is best handled by modularizing the architecture of the software project into uniquely deployable entities. Once the software has been modularized, the deployment and automated testing apparatuses can be broken into multiple component-oriented delivery pipelines. An example of a multi-component delivery pipeline is shown next:

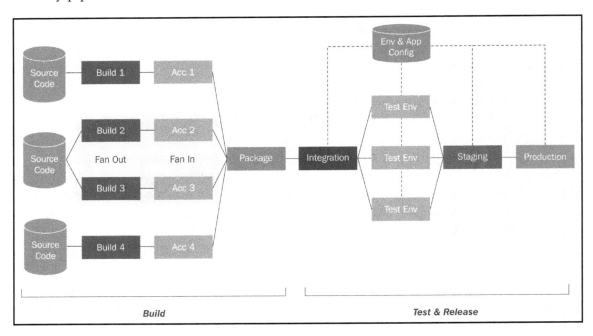

As we can see from the diagram, multiple pipelines can be created in an effort to streamline the deployment process. Each pipeline would have its own build, package, unit test, and related apparatuses. From these multiple pipelines, we can deploy individual component versions into environments swiftly and reliably.

Now that we have a good grasp on how a basic pipeline would be architected, let's take a look at how the same type of pipeline would look in terms of notifications and feedback.

CI->CD feedback loop

The CI feedback loop is one of the major selling points of CI->CD. The basic idea is that the user base and stakeholders can get CD feedback loop almost instantaneous feedback on the quality of committed code. This would allow the developers to address automation-identified issues quickly and will help improve the quality of the overall system. The basic feedback loop would look something like what is shown in the following:

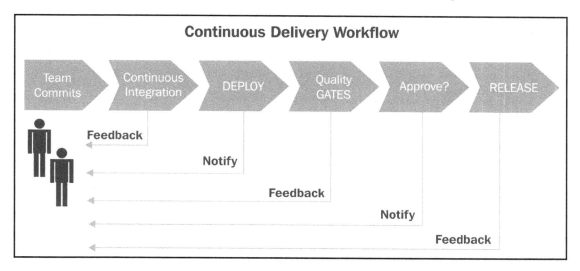

As you can see, the notification loop provides the stakeholders with a notification (e-mail, IM, Slack, Hipchat, and so on) at every stage in the pipeline.

Blue-green deployments

Blue-green deployments represent a wise innovation on the part of system operators and engineering groups. The basic concept of a blue-green deployment is, in many ways, similar to the branching by abstraction concept we discussed earlier.

Blue-green deployments offer the idea of deploying a side-by-side instance of a component or application, all the while leaving the existing instance running and serving live traffic. When the deployment is deemed a success, traffic is flipped from the old version over to the new one. The following is a simple diagram illustrating blue-green deployments:

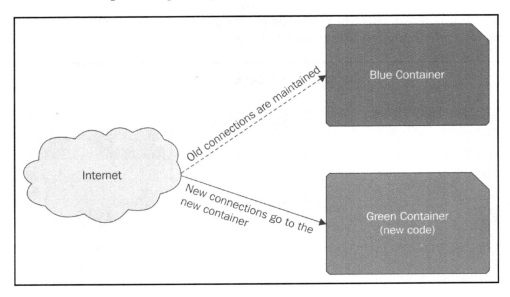

As we can see, new connections go to the green instance and old connections remain persistent with the blue instance.

CI->CD anti-patterns

With all of the talk of CD anti-patterns branching by abstraction and feature toggles it is probably a good idea at CD anti-patterns this point to look at some anti-patterns that are commonly employed by organizations that represent the antithesis of CI->CD best practices:

- **Feature branches**: This is because one of the core tenants of Continuous Integration is the merging of code with the main line. This is the area where defects become most prevalent.

- **Leaving the build in a failed state**: Leaving the build in a known failed state is a common anti-pattern for Continuous Integration efforts. This is an anti-pattern since it effectively leaves a landmine for other developers.
- **Keeping code locally on a developer workstation for long periods of time**: Coding software changes on a local system and not merging it with the mainline is, in essence, hiding changes. The risk from this pattern comes with the huge merge that needs to be done. This large-scale merge usually takes place right before a release, which puts the release quality at risk.

Ansible's Role in CI->CD

Ansible fits in a number of areas of the CI->CD implementation. It can be used for build environment provisioning, local workstation environment provisioning, configuration management on deployment servers, managing physical deployments, and much more.

In this section of Implementing DevOps with Ansible, we will take a look at where Ansible fits into the CI->CD pipeline implementation and some best practices associated with each implementation location. Before we begin looking into focus areas, let's identify the common steps in a CI->CD pipeline.

Initially, a delivery pipeline will be simple; it may contain a set of very basic steps. These steps might include the followng:

1. Check out the source control when a change is committed.
2. Perform a build or syntax check.
3. Execute some unit tests.
4. Report on the quality of the commit.

These steps are illustrated in the following diagram:

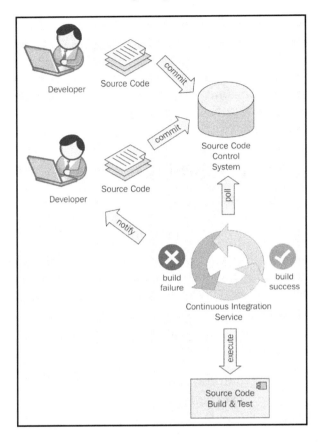

Based on the initial CI process described, we might consider using Ansible in the following CI steps:

- To help developers provision their development environment using an Ansible playbook
- To provision the build machine automatically and ensure the build machine's configuration is maintained by Ansible playbooks
- To act as the automation binding to execute the build and unit tests

As we can see from these set of steps, we can leverage Ansible in more ways than simply to perform configuration management tasks and deployments.

Now that we have Continuous Integration defined, let's take a look at how Ansible can be used within the extension of CI and CD. Take a look at the following Continuous Delivery diagram:

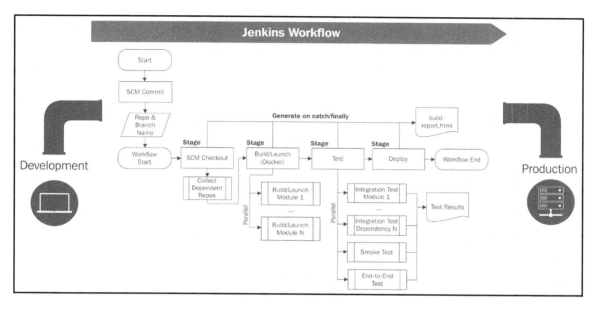

Based on this diagram and flowchart, we can see that there are a number of places within CI->CD where Ansible would prove useful. Let's take a look at these places:

1. In provisioning the test environments (smoke, functional, and unit).
2. In provisioning the deployment environments (DEV, QA, STG, PROD).
3. In performing the deployment.
4. In launching the application after it has been deployed.
5. In rolling back the environment if there are failures.
6. In performing a feathered/incremental rollout of the application into production.

Ansible best practices in CI->CD

Ansible can be leveraged for a number of tasks within a Continuous Integration and Continuous Delivery atmosphere. When adopting Ansible, it makes sense to start with a small footprint and expand it to be more and more responsible for the automation being executed.

In this section, let's take a few minutes to explore some best practices within CI->CD in conjunction with Ansible:

1. Always store your Ansible playbooks in source control.
2. Ship your ansible playbooks with your artifacts (version everything!).
3. Maintain separate inventory files for each environment (DEV, QA, and so on).
4. Try to use the same playbooks for deploying to DEV as you would in production.
5. Leverage Ansible's configuration management implementation to help keep your infrastructure in sync.
6. Keep your playbooks as simple as possible.
7. Use roles to help define reusable automation.
8. Use Ansible for your build and deployment automation glue where possible.
9. Keep your environments in sync (Apples | Apples | Apples, Dev | QA | PROD).

Integrating Ansible with Jenkins

In this section, we will talk about integrating Ansible with Jenkins. Jenkins is a modern CI and automation orchestration solution created and distributed by the open source community. Jenkins originated as Hudson and was eventually transitioned with a new brand name and developed into a comprehensive free and open source build and delivery pipeline orchestration solution. You can download a copy of Jenkins at `https://jenkins.io/`.

Integrating Ansible with Jenkins is generally a straightforward task. To accomplish this, there are a few well-known integration points where Ansible can be leveraged. They include the Jenkins Ansible plugin, installing Ansible on the Jenkins CI server directly and calling it through an execute shell operation and using the Ansible module to control Jenkins. Let's spend a few minutes discussing each of these options and see how they work.

The Jenkins Ansible plugin

The Jenkins Ansible plugin provides the ability for Jenkins to directly communicate with Ansible and run a playbook. This option is probably the most straightforward integration point between Jenkins and Ansible. Using this solution, Ansible doesn't necessarily need to run playbooks on a remote server (however, it definitely can). In this solution, we can run playbooks directly from the Jenkins server and either have those playbooks run locally or run them against targeted infrastructure.

In order to facilitate the execution of playbooks through Jenkins, we will need to first install the Ansible plugin via the Jenkins plugin manager. Let's take a look at how to do this.

 This tutorial assumes you have a Jenkins instance already installed and running.

The first thing we will want to do is fire up Jenkins. Upon the initial load of Jenkins, we will see something like the following:

To install the Ansible plugin. simply navigate to **Plugin Manager** (as a Jenkins administrator) and select **Ansible plugin** from the **Available** plugins tab and install the plugin. This is shown in the following screenshots:

Search for the Ansible plugin and select it. Now install the plugin by clicking on **Install without restart**:

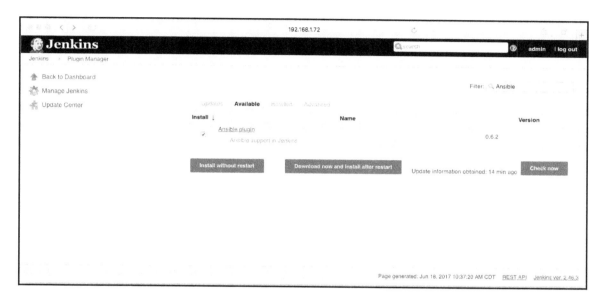

Next, we will want to go to the job configuration page for the job we wish to leverage Ansible through and enable the job to use Ansible. The configuration would look something like what is shown in the following screenshot:

From this screenshot, we can see that there are a number of options available for use with the Ansible plugin in Jenkins. The complete documentation is available at `https://wiki.je nkins-ci.org/display/JENKINS/Ansible+Plugin`.

Once the plugin and job are configured, run the Jenkins job to see it connect to Ansible and leverage Ansible for the automation engine of the job. The output from the execution of a Jenkins job using the Ansible plugin would be something like what is shown in the following screenshot:

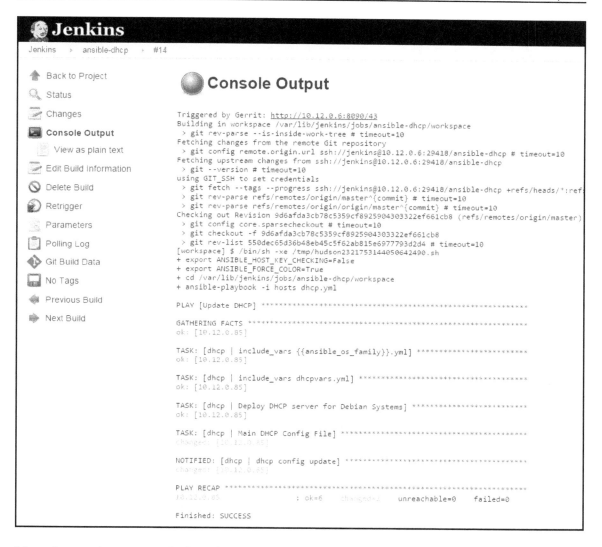

Now that we have a good idea of how to leverage Jenkins to execute Ansible playbook, let's take a look at how to have Ansible control Jenkins via the API.

Ansible playbooks in this scenario are best stored in source control and checked out during the SCM phase of the Jenkins job.

The Jenkins Ansible API modules

The Jenkins Ansible module provides a direct API-level integration between Jenkins and Ansible. Through this solution, Ansible can manage and control Jenkins through its REST API. The Jenkins REST API is fairly robust and provides the ability to create jobs, execute jobs, manage users, and much more. In this section, we will take a look at some examples of the capabilities that the Ansible module provide.

Ansible's integration with Jenkins is broken down into three uniquely classified modules. These modules (as mentioned previously) communicate with Jenkins on an API level and provide a level of control over the Jenkins solution. The three specific modules that we will be looking at are as follows:

- jenkins_job: Manages Jenkins jobs
- jenkins_plugin: Adds or removes the Jenkins plugin
- jenkins_script: Executes a groovy script in the Jenkins instance

Let's start with the jenkins_job Ansible module.

The jenkins_job Ansible Module

The jenkins_job Ansible module provides a level of inter-connectivity between Jenkins jobs and Ansible. Through this module, Ansible can create Jenkins jobs, execute them, manage them, delete them, and more. In order to use this module, we will need the following package libraries installed on the Ansible control server:

- python-jenkins >= 0.4.12
- lxml >= 3.3.3

These libraries can be installed using pip or a package management system such as apt-get or yum.

After making sure the modules are installed, we can begin to make use of the Ansible module's features. Let's take a look at some example playbook plays to create and control Jenkins jobs via the REST API. In addition to this, we will also take a look at the documentation for the supported features of the module:

```
# Create a Jenkins Job
- jenkins_job:
    config: "{{ lookup('file', 'templates/example.xml') }}"
    name: HelloJenkins
    password: admin
```

```
    url: "http://localhost:8080"
    user: admin
```

```
# Delete a jenkins job using the Ansible Jenkins_Job Module
  - jenkins_job:
    name: AnsibleExample
    password: admin
    state: absent
    url: http://localhost:8080
    user: admin
```

```
# Disable a Jenkins job using the Ansible Jenkins_Job module
  - jenkins_job:
    name: AnsibleExample
    password: admin
    enabled: False
    url: http://localhost:8080
    user: admin
```

 To create the `example.xml` template, you will need to use the Jenkins UI wizard to create a new template. This can be done via the job templates plugin. More information on this plugin can be found at the following URL: https://www.cloudbees.com/products/cloudbees-jenkins-platform/enterprise-edition/features/templates-plugin

Integrating Ansible with Vagrant

In this section, we will talk about integrating Ansible with Vagrant. Vagrant is a freely available infrastructure virtualization solution that is currently in use by countless organizations. It is provided free of charge via the kind folks at HashiCorp. A complete documentation for Vagrant can be found at https://www.vagrantup.com/intro/index.html.

To begin, we will assume you already have Vagrant up and running. If not, refer to the instructions located within HashiCorp's Vagrant Up website at https://www.vagrantup.com/docs/cli/up.html to get the initial setup completed. Once the initial setup of Vagrant has been completed, we can take a look at how to leverage Ansible within Vagrant.

Leveraging Ansible for Vagrant provisioning

Ansible's playbook implementation can be used to provision Vagrant machines through the Ansible provider. Providers in Vagrant allow the Vagrant user to specify a configuration management solution that will be leveraged to automate the standup of a given virtual machine. This information is contained in a Ruby Vagrantfile. An example of a simple Vagrantfile is provided here:

```
# This is an example Vagrantfile which can be used with
# Vagrant 1.7 and greater to provision an Ubuntu Box
# using Ansible

Vagrant.require_version ">= 1.7.0"
Vagrant.configure(2) do |config|

config.vm.box = "ubuntu/trusty64"
  config.vm.provision "ansible" do |ansible|
  ansible.verbose = "v"
  ansible.playbook = "playbook.yml"
  end
end
```

From this example, we can see that we use Ansible to configure our Vagrant environment. This will cause Vagrant to execute the Ansible playbook. Once the Vagrantfile has been updated, we can run it using the `vagrant up` command.

Summary

In this chapter, we talked about Continuous Integration, Continuous Delivery, and Ansible. We also talked about the organizational requirements of CI->CD and how CI->CD makes software delivery more efficient. You learned about some of the patterns that make a CI->CD implementation effective.

After talking about CI->CD in depth and discussing the said patterns, we talked about Ansible's role within a CI->CD oriented organization. We discovered the connecting points that tools such as Ansible can be leveraged to make the process more efficient. By standardizing and making a software development organization more efficient through the use of modern tools such as Ansible, we can save the organization time and money.

In the next chapter, we will explore how to use Ansible with Docker. The chapter will teach you how to provision docker containers using Ansible, how to integrate Ansible with dockers service, how to manage docker image facts, and how to gain full control over docker images.

10
Ansible and Docker

Ansible's realm of DevOps integrations is not limited to CI solutions or Configuration Management provisioning implementations. In addition to these, its integration with cloud infrastructure and virtualization-oriented solutions is considered second to none by industry experts. Virtualization solutions such as Docker and Vagrant have taken the cloud computing industry by storm. As such, the integration between Configuration Management tools (including Ansible) has become increasingly robust.

In this chapter, we will take a deep dive into the relationship that can be forged between Docker and Ansible. We will discover how Ansible can be used to create, maintain, and deploy Docker images. We will take a look at how Ansible's module solution for Docker can help automate the delivery of software applications. We will discover commonly popular ways to integrate Ansible with this modern virtualization solution and learn how experts in the industry are combining these two tools to create horizontally scalable and powerful infrastructure delivery solutions.

Upon completing this chapter, we will have a better understanding of how to integrate Ansible with Docker. We will have a solid grasp of the technical requirements required to create a scalable Docker environment, and you will learn how to better automate continuous integration and continuous delivery pipelines.

More specifically, in this chapter, we will cover the following topics:

- Understanding Docker's Architecture
- Managing Docker Containers with Ansible
- Using Ansible to Create Docker Images
- Managing Docker Images with Ansible
- Gathering Facts About Docker Containers using Ansible

Let's get started!

Understanding Docker's Architecture

Initially, combining Docker and Ansible may seem contrary to good configuration management tactics. However, after some research, we quickly learn that these two seemingly different technologies are actually quite robust and scalable when combined. This chapter will focus on integrating Ansible and Docker.

Docker is easily the frontrunner of virtualization solutions. It provides a huge benefit above virtually every other virtualization solution on the market. As such, Dockers popularity has grown significantly in organizations looking to deliver high-quality, robust implementations to customers.

Before we can dive into the integration points, let's talk about Dockers' architecture. This is important to understand as it is what sets Docker aside from the competition. The following diagram shows Docker's unique architecture in detail:

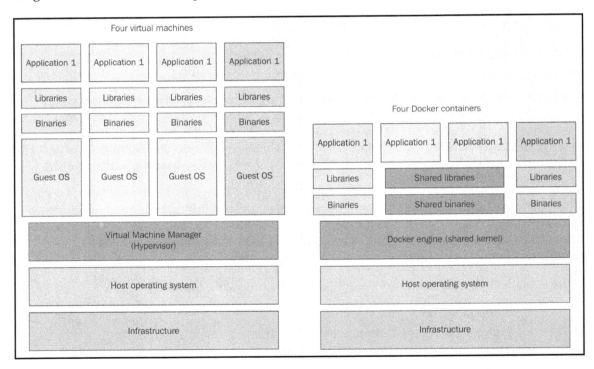

As we can see from the preceding diagram, Dockers architecture provides us with a **shared kernel** that sits on top of the **Host operating system**. In addition to the shared kernel, we also have **Shared libraries** and a set of shared resources.

This is important to understand because in the case of the **Host operating system**, the flavor of Linux is irrelevant. This support structure allows Docker to sit on top of any flavor of Linux and yet still serve up a filesystem from another flavor of Linux. For example, the **Host operating system** could be Ubuntu Linux and yet the containers might have a Fedora flavor.

Let's look at how this works via the following diagram:

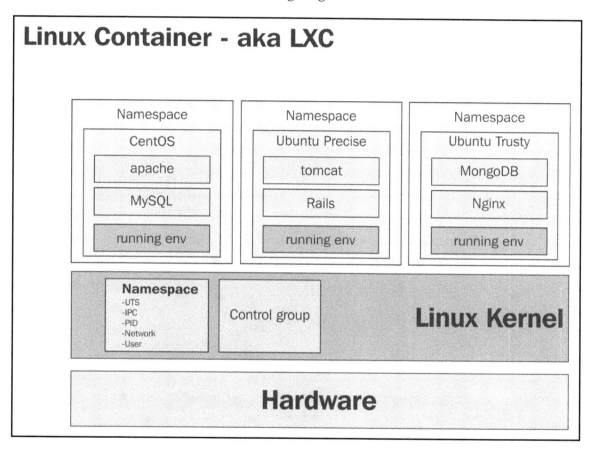

From the preceding diagram, we can see exactly how the various Linux distributions can be used via a Docker container. In our illustration, we have three highly unique flavors of Linux and web applications that reside within different Linux flavors. Neat, right?

Understanding Docker containers as environments

Docker's implementation makes it highly effective for spinning up environments. Environments in this context represent application hosts, database tiers, and APIs that can be combined to provide a working instance of a software solution. In the case of larger organizations, these environments might be multiple instances (development, QA, stage, and production).

In the following diagram, we can see the architecture of a full-scale environment implementation using Docker:

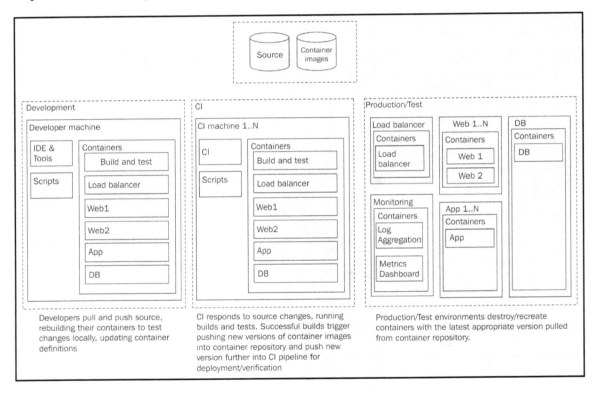

In the preceding diagram, we have multiple containers serving up multiple environments. Ansible's integration and orchestration solution can help pave and maintain these environments. In the next section, we will see exactly how.

Managing Docker Containers with Ansible

Ansible provides a unique set of modules that allow Ansible playbook developers to integrate Ansible with Docker directly. The *Docker module* provides the Ansible playbook developer with the ability to `create`, `start`, `restart`, `modify`, and `remove`.

In this section, we will take a look at basic operational techniques that can be applied to managing Docker containers using Ansible. Specifically, we will cover:

- How to create Docker containers using Ansible
- How to update Docker containers using Ansible
- How to delete Docker containers using Ansible
- How to launch a Docker container using Ansible

Initially, performing these tasks may seem a bit daunting. But once we pull back the veil on this solution, we will see that the implementation of such tasks within a playbook is fairly straightforward. Let's take a look at how these playbook modules can help us manage Docker containers.

Creating Docker containers

Creating Docker containers may seem like a difficult task through Ansible; however, it's actually quite simple. In this section, you will learn how to do exactly that. Let's get started:

```
- name: Create a data container
  docker_container:
    name: mydata
    image: busybox
    volumes:
      - /data
```

The preceding Ansible task creates a Docker data container using the `busybox` image with a simple volume of `/data`. While it's easy to create simple containers, we will obviously need more substance to create more useful containers. Let's take a look at how to do this.

Removing Docker containers

Removing Docker containers can be achieved with a simple Ansible state for the container provided within the task itself. The following is an example of how to remove a Docker container from the local Docker registry:

```
- name: Remove MYSQL container
  docker_container:
    name: mysql
    state: absent
```

Launching and stopping Docker containers

Launching Docker containers using Ansible can be achieved via the Ansible Docker task. In the following example, we launch a Docker container for `mysql`. Let's take a look:

```
# The following task launches a mysql docker container
- name: MySQL Database Container Launch
  docker:
  name: database
  image: mysql:1.0
  state: started
```

From the preceding example, we can see the task launches a MySQL Docker container (version 1.0). The primary parameters we used in this task are `image` and `name`. These parameters define the image and tag for the task to use and what we want to title the container we are managing.

The key to launching the container is the `started` state. State in this context provides the following switches:

- `absent`
- `present`
- `stopped`
- `started`

So, in order to expand on this, let's take a look at an example of the same Ansible task, which instead of launching the container will stop it:

```
# The following task stops a mysql docker container
- name: MySQL Database Container Stop
  docker:
  name: database
```

```
image: mysql:1.0
state: stopped
```

For teams who update their containers frequently, it is probably a good idea to add the following flags to the Docker container launch operation:

```
pull: always
```

These operational parameters will force Docker to pull a fresh container every time it's executed *and* to reload the container as part of the task.

For a complete documentation of the Ansible Docker container module, go to `https://docs` `.ansible.com/ansible/docker_container_module.html`.

In addition to launching and stopping a Docker container using the `started` and `stopped` switches, we can also launch a container and execute a command. Let's take a look at how to do this:

```
- name: Starting a container and executing a command
  docker_container:
  name: sleepy
  image: ubuntu:14.04
  command: ["sleep", "infinity"]
```

Managing network access Docker containers

What good is an isolated Docker container with no network access? In this section, we are going to take a look at how to add a container to a network and conversely also remove it from the network.

To manage network connectivity within a Docker container, the Ansible task implementation has provided a set of network switches to the main Docker container task. Let's take a look at an example of these switches in action and see how to leverage Ansible in this form.

Adding a container to a network can be done using the following code:

```
- name: Add container to CoprLAN and GuestLan networks
  docker_container:
  name: sleepy
  networks:

- name: CorpLan
  ipv4_address: 172.1.10.1
  links:
```

```
    - sleeper
    - name: GuestLan
  ipv4_address: 172.1.10.2
```

Removing a container from the network can be done using the following code:

```
- name: Remove container from the CorpLan network
  docker_container:
  name: MySQL
  networks:
    - name: CorpLan
  purge_networks: yes
```

Using Ansible to Create Docker Images

Docker provides an out-of-box solution to build Docker images using a Docker domain-specific language. Docker files are created in order to provide spin-up instructions that Docker can execute in order to build an image. After learning to create Docker files, one may ask why we would advocate for leveraging Ansible to create Docker containers in conjunction with a Dockerfile. The answer is quite simple—idempotency. An idempotent operation is one where the operation, once executed, can be executed repeatedly without any change. This is precisely what Ansible does.

Once Ansible has effected a change in a given system, it will automatically skip that change if the change is already present. So for example, if an Ansible playbook runs against a target system and makes, say, four changes to that system, it will automatically skip trying to make that change again *if* the change is found already present or if the system is already in the desired state.

In terms of creating Docker images using Ansible, it is a good idea to leverage Ansible because the domain language is a bit easier to read, the operations are idempotent, and the changes can be applied to one container or a hundred simultaneously. This provides a large amount of flexibility and scalability within this space. In this section, we are going to look at how to leverage Ansible to create Docker images. Let's get started.

Using Dockerfiles to launch Ansible playbooks

By leveraging Docker files to call Ansible playbooks once launched, we can make our implementation of Docker containers fairly robust. This type of implementation has a number of benefits. The most notable are as follows:

- If there is existing infrastructure that is already leveraging Ansible, keeping the automation control consistent is a no-brainer
- Ansible's module system provides integration with a number of third-party tools and technologies
- Ansible's implementation of easy-to-read syntax and idempotent architecture provides a significant set of capabilities for developers onboarding into Ansible.

In this section, we will take a look at how to best leverage a Dockerfile to execute an Ansible playbook. Let's get started by taking a look at an example Dockerfile:

```
# This DOCKERFILE creates a docker image with Ubuntu 14.04 and Ansible
installed
# It also executes a playbook upon startup
FROM ansible/ubuntu14.04-ansible:stable

# This Defines the location for Ansible playbooks as /srv/example
ADD ansible /srv/example
WORKDIR /srv/example

# Execute Ansible with the playbook's primary entry point as myplaybook.yml
RUN ansible-playbook myplaybook.yml -c local
CMD ["--help"]
```

The preceding example should be fairly self-documented. However, it basically creates a Docker image based on Ubuntu 14.04, defines a working directory for Ansible, and then runs Ansible locally using `myplaybook.yml` as its source. Easy, right?

Managing Docker Images with Ansible

Docker images are slightly different from containers. That is, the image is the stored copy of the container. Docker images are stored in what is commonly referred to as a **registry.** In the context of Docker, the registry acts similar to a source control solution in many ways. That source control solution is mirrored in many ways to Git. Docker registries parallel Git in many ways; the most obvious is the ability to have a distributed set of registries. Confused yet? Let's take a look at the following diagram:

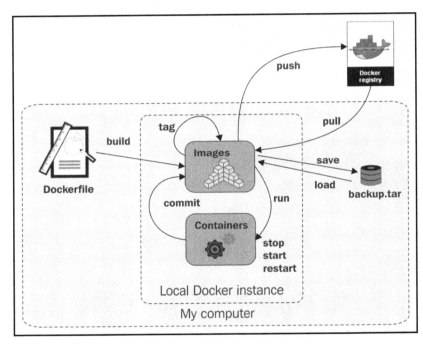

From the preceding illustration, we can see that the **Docker registry** is a remote location that stores Docker images. Docker images then reside in a local registry (local to the developer) where they can manipulate and store changes made to the various containers stored within the **Docker registry**. When a set of changes has been deemed complete, the developer has the option to **push** the image(s) to the remote registry and communicate their changes.

Pulling, pushing, and tagging images

One of the fundamental Docker development requirements is the ability of the developer to pull, push, and tag Docker images from the remote registry. Ansible can be useful in this *if* you have a build system that orchestrates changes to the infrastructure and stores the baked images for future deployment. Within this type of scenario, the workflow might go something like this:

1. The developer checks out the source code for a set of Ansible playbooks that define the organization's infrastructure.
2. The developer makes a change to a playbook that is associated with the DB tier of the environment and commits their code change to Git.
3. Jenkins offers an automated CI solution, which sees the commit, and pulls down the playbook repo for validation.
4. Jenkins executes Ansible to run the playbook, which automatically creates a newer version of the Docker image.
5. The updated Docker image is then pushed to the remote registry for deployment into a development or QA environment.

This type of workflow is pretty simple. It ensures that the development organization is not manually making changes to the containers; it ensures that Ansible is the tool used to develop, automate, and deploy the software solution; and it ensures that the images spun up are tested before deployment to production.

Automating this type of workflow in Ansible takes the ability to pull a Docker image, push a Docker image, and tag a Docker image. Let's look at the playbook tasks that could make this happen.

To pull a Docker image, use the following code:

```
- name: Pull a Docker Image
  docker_image:
    name: pacur/centos-7
```

To tag an image and push it, use the following code:

```
- name: Tag a Docker Image and Push to docker hub
  docker_image:
    name: pacur/centos-7
    repository: myorg/myimage
    tag: 1.1
    push: yes
```

As we can see, the implementation of these tasks is actually *very* straightforward. But what about tagging and pushing to a local registry? I'm glad you asked. Let's look at how to do that:

```
- name: Tag a Docker Image and push to the local registry
  docker_image:
  name: MyCentOS
  repository: localhost:5000/mycentos
  tag: 1.0
  push: yes
```

Easy, right? Finally, let's look at how to build and image from a Dockerfile and push it to a private registry. This should be simple, easy right?

The following example shows how an image is built from a Dockerfile:

```
- name: Build a Docker Image from a Dockerfile and push it to a private
  registry
  docker_image:
  path: ./test
  name: registry.myorg.com/foo/test
  tag: v1
  push: yes
```

This task assumes you have a Dockerfile located at ./test, and it definitely isn't rocket science.

Building and archiving Docker images

Building Docker images from a Dockerfile is a topic we briefly touched on in the previous section, but it deserves a bit more depth. In building a Docker image from a Dockerfile, we can leverage it later. But first, we would need a Dockerfile to make this happen. Let's look at an example of a Dockerfile and then look at how to build it using Ansible:

```
# This DOCKERFILE creates a docker image with Ubuntu 14.04 and Ansible
installed
# It also executes a playbook upon startup
FROM ansible/ubuntu14.04-ansible:stable

# This Defines the location for Ansible playbooks as /srv/example
ADD ansible /srv/example
WORKDIR /srv/example

# Execute Ansible with the playbook's primary entry point as myplaybook.yml
RUN ansible-playbook myplaybook.yml -c local
```

```
CMD ["--help"]
```

This Dockerfile should look *very* familiar. In fact, it is! It's the source code we leveraged earlier to have it run an Ansible playbook at launch. Can you see where we are going with this example? Save this Dockerfile to the /opt/test directory and then create a playbook with the following contents:

```
---
- hosts: all
  remote_user: root
  tasks:
    - name: Build Docker Image
      docker_image:
      path: /opt/test
      name: myimage
```

Now create a simple playbook in /srv/example/myplaybook.yml with the following content:

```
---
- hosts: all
  tasks:
    - name: Installs nginx web server on a Docker Image
      apt: pkg=nginx state=installed update_cache=true
      notify:
        - start nginx

handlers:
 - name: start nginx
   service: name=nginx state=started
```

Nice. Now run the /opt/test Ansible playbook and see the solution build a Docker container with nginx already installed and sitting happily in the local Docker registry.

Saving and loading archived Docker images

Docker provides a unique ability to share containers using tarballs. This allows developers to pass around a tarball copy of the infrastructure for inspection and manipulation. Generally, there are two distinct operations involved in archiving a Docker container (exporting/archiving and loading an archive); a Docker image is also a really straightforward task. Let's look at an example code on how to archive a Docker image:

```
Archiving an Image:
- name: Archive A Docker Image as a TAR file
  docker_image:
  name: registry.ansible.com/foo/sinatra
```

```
tag: v1
archive_path: sinatra.tar
```

Loading an archived image can be done using the following code:

```
- name: Load a Docker Image from a TAR archive and push to a private
registry
  docker_image:
  name: localhost:5000/foo/sinatra
  tag: v1
  push: yes
  load_path: sinatra.tar
```

Gathering Facts About Docker Containers

Facts are the bread and butter of how Ansible works and manages information about its controlled/automated systems. Facts represent data about the device and the current state. Ansible provides a set of playbook tasks that can be readily leveraged to gather facts about Docker images. Let's take a look at a couple of examples of how to accomplish this.

This is example 1:

```
- name: Inspect a single Docker image
  docker_image_facts:
  name: foo/centos-7
```

This is example 2:

```
- name: Inspect multiple Docker images
  docker_image_facts:
  name:
  - foo/centos-7
  - sinatra
```

The preceding playbook tasks inspect a single or multiple Docker image setup and report the facts. The fact data itself is stored in the return value. An example of the output is provided as follows:

```
[{'Container':
'e83a452b8fb8ff43oj094j4050131ca5c863629a47639530d9ad2008d610', 'Name':
'registry:2', 'Author': '', 'GraphDriver': {'Data': None, 'Name': 'aufs'},
'Architecture': 'amd64', 'VirtualSize': 165808884, 'ContainerConfig':
{'Cmd': ['/bin/sh', '-c', '#(nop) CMD
["/etc/docker/registry/config.yml"]'], 'Env':
['PATH=/usr/local/sbin:/usr/local/bin:/usr/sbin:/usr/bin:/sbin:/bin'],
'StdinOnce': False, 'Hostname': 'e5c68db50333', 'WorkingDir': '',
```

```
'Entrypoint': ['/bin/registry'], 'Volumes': {'/var/lib/registry': {}},
'OnBuild': [], 'OpenStdin': False, 'Tty': False, 'Domainname': '', 'Image':
'c72dce2618dc8groeirgjeori444c2b1e64e0205ead5befc294f8111da23bd6a2c799',
'Labels': {}, 'ExposedPorts': {'5000/tcp': {}}, 'User': '', 'AttachStdin':
False, 'AttachStderr': False, 'AttachStdout': False}, 'Os': 'linux',
'RepoTags': ['registry:2'], 'Comment': '', 'DockerVersion': '1.9.1',
'Parent':
'f0b1f729f784b755e7bf9c8c2e65d8a0a35a533769c2588f02895f6781ac0805',
'Config': {'Cmd': ['/etc/docker/registry/config.yml'], 'Env':
['PATH=/usr/local/sbin:/usr/local/bin:/usr/sbin:/usr/bin:/sbin:/bin'],
'StdinOnce': False, 'Hostname': 'e5c68db50333', 'WorkingDir': '',
'Entrypoint': ['/bin/registry'], 'Volumes': {'/var/lib/registry': {}},
'OnBuild': [], 'OpenStdin': False, 'Tty': False, 'Domainname': '', 'Image':
'c72dce2618dc409834095834jt4ggf5ead5befc294f8111da23bd6a2c799', 'Labels':
{}, 'ExposedPorts': {'5000/tcp': {}}, 'User': '', 'AttachStdin': False,
'AttachStderr': False, 'AttachStdout': False}, 'Created':
'2016-03-08T21:08:15.399680378Z', 'RepoDigests': [], 'Id':
'53773d8552f07b7340958340fj32094jfd67b344141d965463a950a66e08', 'Size': 0}]
```

The output of the command provides a nice hash data set. This data could then be further dissected and used within playbook's.

Summary

In this chapter, we discovered some interesting and unique ways to integrate the Ansible automation system with Docker. We learned that these two seemingly redundant technologies can be combined to provide a robust automation implementation that scales very well.

We also talked about how to inversely leverage Ansible playbook tasks to create, update, delete, and manage containers. Then, we covered how to attach and remove networking from these containers. You learned that even though these implementations might have looked difficult at first, they proved to be quite easy actually.

In the next chapter, we will take a look at how to extend Ansible and create custom modules. We will educate you on how to use Python to extend Ansible and create custom modules that integrate with unique specific technology stacks. This will be done by providing a set of tutorials that teach you how to write and release custom Ansible modules. This chapter will teach you how to read input, manage facts, perform automated tasks, interact with REST APIs, and generate documentation.

11
Extending Ansible

Ansible has matured over the years to support a wide variety of technologies, tools, operating systems, and processes. Its flexible architecture and modular implementation make it ideal for DevOps oriented groups with varying or diverse requirements. The extensible architecture that comprises Ansible was designed to support the creation of modules and expand the Ansible solution to fit the user's needs. As a result, Ansible itself and many of its now core modules derive from once available plugins.

Throughout the years, Ansible's creators added numerous API hooks and architectures in an effort to support expanding Ansible itself via a wide variety of means. The end result of this effort was a highly extensible system, which was leveraged by developers to create a significant amounts of additional core functionality. A plugin system!

Over the years, the Ansible plugin and module system have expanded out and taken a more central role in Ansible's core architecture. The once clumsily conglomerated extension system has been refined into a well-architected and implemented plugin solution. The once haphazardly implemented extension points have been refined to become a robust and highly capable module API. As a result of these improvements, the plugin and module systems have evolved significantly since its infantile stages.

In this chapter, we are going to take a tour of the Ansible module and plugin architecture. We are going to explore the inner workings of the Ansible architecture and APIs. We are going to dive into Python development and leverage it to create some custom modules and plugin extensions that will enhance our Ansible implementations to support custom needs. Specifically, we will cover the following topics:

- Understanding Ansible Plugins and its Architecture
- Setting Up the Ansible Module Development Environment
- Developing a HelloWorld Ansible Module and Extending it
- Setting Up a Plugin Development Environment
- Understanding the Different Types of Plugins

As we embark on this quest to learn about the Ansible plugin system, take careful note of the syntax and formatting to ensure the code is kept clean and unambiguous. By following this general rule of thumb, you will learn how to create and deliver high-quality Ansible extensions. Let's get started.

Understanding Ansible Plugins and its Architecture

Ansible's implementation is highly modular. A modular architecture provides a high level of encapsulation (keeping concerns segregated and preventing them from cross-contaminating). The plugin solution within Ansible's subsystems is architected in order to keep additions organized and encapsulated. This architecture is divided into distinct subsystems. The most critical subsystems for Ansible plugins and modules and modules are defined as follows:

- The Ansible Core modules
- Ansible configs
- Custom modules
- The Ansible Python API

To better describe the vague list just provided, the following diagram provides an illustrated view of the Ansible architecture:

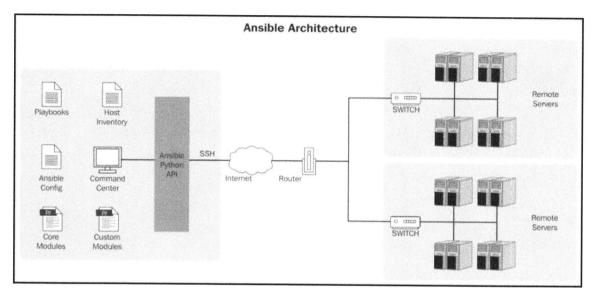

The preceding diagram highlights three of the most critical subsystems for Ansible plugin and module development. The **Core Modules**, the **Custom Modules**, and the **Ansible Python API**. This stack provides a comprehensive set of components for extending Ansible.

In Ansible, there are two distinct ways to extend the Ansible Core solution. These are described as follows:

- **Ansible plugins**: Plugins in Ansible extend the core functionality of the master system and provide additional functionality to the control server.
- **Ansible modules:** Modules in Ansible extend the capabilities of playbooks running on target systems. These would be the systems that Ansible runs its playbooks on.

These two distinctions are quite important as it defines the scope of the development. Let's take a look at a simple Ansible playbook so we can better understand the role Ansible modules play within the Ansible architecture:

```
# This simple playbook installs / updates Apache
---
- hosts: all
  tasks:
    - name: Ensure Apache is installed and at the latest version
      yum: name=httpd state=latest
```

Based on the preceding playbook, can you determine how modules are used? No? Let's examine this playbook more closely:

```
# This simple playbook installs / updates Apache
---
- hosts: all
  tasks:
    - name: Ensure Apache is installed and at the latest version
      <yum>: <param>=<value> <param>=<value>
```

If you guessed that the module name is <yum>, you would be correct. Tasks represented in the playbook form are simply module calls. If this is the case, then we would logically ask ourselves "When should I create my own modules?"

When should we create a module?

The most obvious question at this point is when and why you would want to develop your own Ansible modules. The answer is most of the time you actually won't want to. But there are cases where you may need to. Some examples of this are as follows:

- When communication with a specific API feels clumsy or arduous
- To do something custom that Ansible does not have native support for
- To communicate with an internal process or software that does not have an already developed Ansible module

Generally, if you want to write an Ansible module and the software solution was created by a third-party (open source, commercial, and so on), it makes sense to check the Ansible modules for out-of-the-box support before jumping in and writing code.

In the next section, we will take a look at how to set up the Ansible development environment, where the Ansible module code should be stored and how it should be organized. Let's proceed, shall we?

Setting Up the Ansible Module Development Environment

In this section, we will discuss how to set up a local Linux environment for Ansible module development. In our specific implementation, we will look at how to do this in Ubuntu. However, the same set of configuration options should work under other Linux flavors as well. As new Ansible module developers, we will want to begin by understanding how to configure our system to best support Ansible development, how to setup the modules path, and how to configure the environment for testing.

The first step to getting a development environment up and running is to understand the Ansible library path on the system. This path is where Ansible will search for additional libraries. The default value for the library path is defined within the primary Ansible configuration file (`/etc/ansible/ansible.cfg`). The line item is shown as follows:

```
library = /usr/share/ansible
```

While the default path is defined within the Ansible configuration file, it can be manipulated at runtime by specifying the `--module-path` on the command line when launching Ansible.

In addition to the `--module-path` switch, we can also override the default modules path via a system-level environment variable. An example of how to do this is provided next:

```
#> export
ANSIBLE_LIBRARY=/srv/modules/custom_modules:/srv/modules/vendor_modules
```

When developing and using Ansible modules, the most preferred location to store the modules is next to the playbook itself within a `./library` directory. This would involve creating a directory structure that looks like the following:

```
#> foo.yml
 #> library/
 #> library/mymodule.py
```

Within the preceding structure, we could leverage the tasks available within the playbook. Pretty nice, right? These are the basics of setting up the development environment using Ansible. From here, we should probably also set up some basic debugging and lint solutions.

Ansible module testing tool setup

Ansible developers have implemented and released a pretty helpful tool to debug syntax and format issues within Ansible plugins and modules. This linter is quite useful indeed. To install the linter, execute the following command:

```
$ pip install git+https://github.com/sivel/ansible-
testing.git#egg=ansible_testing
```

Upon executing the preceding command, we should see the following output:

```
jmcallister@ubuntu:~$ sudo pip install git+https://github.com/sivel/ansible-testing.git#eg=ansible_t
_testing
[sudo] password for jmcallister:
The directory '/home/jmcallister/.cache/pip/http' or its parent directory is not owned by the curren
t user and the cache has been disabled. Please check the permissions and owner of that directory. If
executing pip with sudo, you may want sudo's -H flag.
The directory '/home/jmcallister/.cache/pip' or its parent directory is not owned by the current use
r and caching wheels has been disabled. check the permissions and owner of that directory. If execut
ing pip with sudo, you may want sudo's -H flag.
Collecting git+https://github.com/sivel/ansible-testing.git#eg=ansible_t_testing
  Cloning https://github.com/sivel/ansible-testing.git to /tmp/pip-EfzvKW-build
Requirement already satisfied (use --upgrade to upgrade): ansible in /usr/lib/python2.7/dist-package
s (from ansible-testing===0.0.1b0)
Collecting voluptuous==0.8.8 (from ansible-testing===0.0.1b0)
  Downloading voluptuous-0.8.8.tar.gz
Collecting mock (from ansible-testing===0.0.1b0)
  Downloading mock-2.0.0-py2.py3-none-any.whl (56kB)
    100% |                                | 61kB 13kB/s
Requirement already satisfied (use --upgrade to upgrade): setuptools>=0.6b1 in /usr/lib/python2.7/di
st-packages (from voluptuous==0.8.8->ansible-testing===0.0.1b0)
Requirement already satisfied (use --upgrade to upgrade): six>=1.9 in /usr/lib/python2.7/dist-packag
es (from mock->ansible-testing===0.0.1b0)
Collecting funcsigs>=1; python_version < "3.3" (from mock->ansible-testing===0.0.1b0)
  Downloading funcsigs-1.0.2-py2.py3-none-any.whl
Collecting pbr>=0.11 (from mock->ansible-testing===0.0.1b0)
  Downloading pbr-3.1.1-py2.py3-none-any.whl (99kB)
    100% |                                | 102kB 16kB/s
Installing collected packages: voluptuous, funcsigs, pbr, mock, ansible-testing
  Running setup.py install for voluptuous ... done
  Running setup.py install for ansible-testing ... done
Successfully installed ansible-testing-0.0.1b0 funcsigs-1.0.2 mock-2.0.0 pbr-3.1.1 voluptuous-0.8.8
You are using pip version 8.1.1, however version 9.0.1 is available.
You should consider upgrading via the 'pip install --upgrade pip' command.
jmcallister@ubuntu:~$ _
```

Now that we have the lint tool installed, let's check it out to make sure it's installed. Try the following command:

```
#> ansible-validate-modules
```

By executing the preceding command, we should see the following output on the console:

Nice, right? From here, we will want to set up the Ansible module test solution. Let's proceed.

Developing Hello World Ansible Module

Now that we have a basic development environment setup, we are going to explore how to create Ansible modules by taking a look at the obligatory Hello World Ansible module implementation. By creating a Hello World module, we can get our feet wet in Ansible module development and learn the basic structures required for a successful implementation. Let's get started!

To begin our *Hello World* module, let's create a directory structure that reflects the following screenshot:

```
[jmcallister@ubuntu:/opt/ch11$ tree

├── library
│   └── helloworld.py
└── myplaybook.yml

1 directory, 2 files
jmcallister@ubuntu:/opt/ch11$ _
```

Once this structure has been created, let's begin filling in our Ansible Hello World module code. To accomplish this, alter the `helloworld.py` file to contain the following Python code:

```python
#!/usr/bin/python
# The following Python code converts a simple "Hello Ansible" message into
a json object
# for use with an Ansible module call

import json

message = "Hello Ansible"
print(json.dumps({
  "Message" : message
}))
```

Once the preceding code has been implemented, we will want an efficient way to test its functionality. Let's get that testing environment set up next.

Testing a developmental Ansible module

Once the primary Ansible module development environment has been set up, we will want to set up the Ansible module testing environment. This solution will provide us with the ability to validate our Python code without using Ansible directly. As such, it will make the development and validation of potential modules more efficient. To set this up, execute the following commands within the development modules directory:

```
#> git clone git://github.com/ansible/ansible.git
#> source ansible/hacking/env-setup
```

Upon executing these commands, you should see something similar to the following output:

```
jmcallister@ubuntu:/opt/ch11$ sudo git clone git://github.com/ansible/ansible.git
[sudo] password for jmcallister:
Cloning into 'ansible'...
remote: Counting objects: 270173, done.
remote: Compressing objects: 100% (55/55), done.
remote: Total 270173 (delta 32), reused 20 (delta 8), pack-reused 270109
Receiving objects: 100% (270173/270173), 77.68 MiB | 587.00 KiB/s, done.
Resolving deltas: 100% (172171/172171), done.
Checking connectivity... done.
jmcallister@ubuntu:/opt/ch11$ ls
ansible  library  myplaybook.yml
jmcallister@ubuntu:/opt/ch11$ source ansible/hacking/env-setup
running egg_info
creating lib/ansible.egg-info
error: could not create 'lib/ansible.egg-info': Permission denied

Setting up Ansible to run out of checkout...

PATH=/opt/ch11/ansible/bin:/opt/ch11/ansible/test/runner:/home/jmcallister/bin:/home/jmcallister/.lo
cal/bin:/usr/local/sbin:/usr/local/bin:/usr/sbin:/usr/bin:/sbin:/bin:/usr/games:/usr/local/games:/sn
ap/bin
PYTHONPATH=/opt/ch11/ansible/lib:
MANPATH=/opt/ch11/ansible/docs/man:

Remember, you may wish to specify your host file with -i

Done!

jmcallister@ubuntu:/opt/ch11$
```

Once this has been completed, we should have access to a new command, which will enable our ability to test our partially developed Ansible modules. Let's check that out:

```
#> ansible/hacking/test-module -m ./library/helloworld.py
```

The following screenshot shows the output for the preceding command:

```
jmcallister@ubuntu:/opt/ch11$ ansible/hacking/test-module -m ./library/helloworld.py
* including generated source, if any, saving to: /home/jmcallister/.ansible_module_generated
************************************
RAW OUTPUT
{"Message": "Hello Ansible"}


************************************
PARSED OUTPUT
{
    "Message": "Hello Ansible"
}
jmcallister@ubuntu:/opt/ch11$
```

If something were to go wrong (a typo or non-compilable script), we would see something like the following:

```
jmcallister@ubuntu:/opt/ch11$ ansible/hacking/test-module -m ./library/helloworld.py
* including generated source, if any, saving to: /home/jmcallister/.ansible_module_generated
************************************
RAW OUTPUT

Traceback (most recent call last):
  File "/home/jmcallister/.ansible_module_generated", line 6, in <module>
    print(json.dumps({"Message" : message}))
NameError: name 'message' is not defined


************************************
INVALID OUTPUT FORMAT

Traceback (most recent call last):
  File "ansible/hacking/test-module", line 218, in runtest
    results = json.loads(out)
  File "/usr/lib/python2.7/json/__init__.py", line 339, in loads
    return _default_decoder.decode(s)
  File "/usr/lib/python2.7/json/decoder.py", line 364, in decode
    obj, end = self.raw_decode(s, idx=_w(s, 0).end())
  File "/usr/lib/python2.7/json/decoder.py", line 382, in raw_decode
    raise ValueError("No JSON object could be decoded")
ValueError: No JSON object could be decoded
jmcallister@ubuntu:/opt/ch11$ _
```

Reading input parameters

One of the fundamental values that Ansible provides is its connection to the YAML playbooks. Developing modules is useful only if we can create playbooks that pass data parameters to the modules. In this section, you will learn how to expand our Hello World Ansible module to accept and process input parameters from playbooks. We will also look at how to structure our module so that it conforms to the Ansible boilerplate template system designed for module development.

In order for our Hello World program to be able to read input parameters from an Ansible playbook, we will need to modify it a bit. Let's update the `./library/HelloWorld.py` file to the following:

```python
#!/usr/bin/python#!/usr/bin/python
import json
def main():

    module = AnsibleModule(argument_spec=dict( param1 = dict(required=True,
type='str') ) )
    message = module.params['param1']

    print(json.dumps({
        "Message" : message
    }))

    module.exit_json(changed=True, keyword=value)
    module.exit_json(changed=False, msg='error message ', keyword=value)

from ansible.module_utils.basic import *
if __name__ = '__main__':
    main()
```

Next, create a simple playbook `myplaybook.yml` in the parent folder of the library folder with the contents defined as follows:

```yaml
- name: Hello World
  hosts: localhost
  connection: local
  tasks:
    - name: Tell the Ansible Community Hello
      helloworld: param1=hello
```

Once saved, let's execute it and see the output. The following is the command to run and the expected output:

```
#> ansible-playbook myplaybook.yml -i localhost -v
```

The output would look like what is shown in the following screenshot:

Nice, right? Next, let's take a look at what each of these Hello World lines does. The following is a far more documented copy of the helloworld.py script:

```python
#!/usr/bin/python


#Main Entry point for the module
def main():

    # Instantiate the message variable (this will contain our YAML param
value)
    message = ''

    # Instantiate the Ansible Module which will retrieve the value of our
param1 variable
    module = AnsibleModule(argument_spec=dict(param1 = dict(required=True,
type='str')))

    # Set the value of Message to the value of module.params['param1']
    message = module.params['param1']
```

```
    # Display the content of the message in JSON format
    print(json.dumps({"Message": message{))

    # Exit the program SUCCESS/FAIL
    module.exit_json(changed=True, keyword=value)
    module.exit_json(changed=False, msg='error message', keyword=value)

# Import ansible functionality from Ansible.module
from ansible.module_utils.basic import *

# This line imports the functionality of JSON. It allows us to print the
JSON formatted message
import json

# Call Main Function IF _main_ is defined
if __name__ = '__main__':
    main()
```

Adding custom facts to a module

Ansible facts (as we mentioned in earlier chapters) provide informational data points about the systems that have run a playbook or task. At some point, we might need to set some Ansible facts and return them to the Ansible control server. In this section, we will discuss how to set Ansible facts within our Hello World module and some of the limitations of Ansible facts.

According to the Ansible documentation (`https://docs.ansible.com/ansible/dev_guide/developing_modules_general.html`):

> *The setup - Gathers facts about remote hosts module that ships with Ansible provides many variables about a system that can be used in playbooks and templates. However, it's possible to also add your own facts without modifying the system module. To do this, just have the module return a ansible_facts key, like so, along with other return data.*

In this section, we will go over how to gather module-specific custom facts and return them to the Ansible control server. To begin, we will want to define a set of formatted facts. Let's take a look at an example of the code that does this:

```
ansible_facts_dict = {
  "changed" : true,
  "rc" : 5,
  "ansible_facts" : {
  "foo" : "bar",
  }
```

```
}
    module.exit_json(changed=False, result="success",ansible_facts)
```

Based on the previous code, we can see that Ansible facts can be set in the JSON dictionary form and then passed through the `module.exit_json` file. These facts can then be accessed later within the playbook but only after the task that sets the facts has been executed. Nice, right?

Setting up the Ansible Plugin Development Environment

Ansible plugins, as we mentioned earlier, represent actions that are executed on the master (control server) instead of the target host. These plugins allow us to add additional functionality to the Ansible solution easily. Once the plugin has been written, the action is then available to be called via a traditional YAML playbook *action*. Before we start coding our action plugin, let's take a look at how to set up the development environment.

Similar to the modules' development environment, action plugins must reside either in `./<type of plugin>_plugins` next to the playbook being executed *or* within one of the specified folders. For example, you might have a directory structure like the following:

```
#> foo.yml
#> action_plugins/
#> action_plugin/mymodule.py
```

Or, you may have this:

```
#> foo.yml
#> callback_plugins/
#> callback_plugin/mymodule.py
```

Or, you might consider altering the `<type of plugin>_plugins` path in the config folder, as follows:

```
#action_plugins     = /usr/share/ansible/plugins/action
#callback_plugins   = /usr/share/ansible/plugins/callback
#connection_plugins = /usr/share/ansible/plugins/connection
#lookup_plugins     = /usr/share/ansible/plugins/lookup
#vars_plugins       = /usr/share/ansible/plugins/vars
#filter_plugins     = /usr/share/ansible/plugins/filter
#test_plugins       = /usr/share/ansible/plugins/test
```

It is important to uncomment in the configuration the type of plugin you wish to leverage within the config. Once the development environment has been created for the type of plugin we wish to create, it's time to start coding the plugin itself.

Understanding the Different Types of Plugins

Ansible provides the option to create numerous types of plugins. Each plugin type interacts with the Ansible system in a different way. In this section, we will be looking at the different types of plugins available within the Ansible plugin architecture and discover how to code them. The different types of plugins available are as follows:

- Action plugins
- Callback plugins
- Connection plugins
- Lookup plugins
- Vars plugins
- Filter plugins
- Test plugins

In the coming sections, we will take a look at how to code each plugin type and what they are capable of. Let's get started.

Action plugins

In this section, we will take a look at action plugins and you will learn what action plugins do and some basic code examples on how to create new actions that are available within the Ansible subsystems. In Ansible, `action_plugins` are a special type of module that provide additional functionality to an existing module. As we mentioned earlier, `action_plugins` run on the master instead of on the target.

For example, an action plugin represented via an Ansible playbook would look like the following:

```
- name: Special Action to be run on the master
  action: myaction foo=bar
```

The code for such an action plugin might look something like the following:

```python
#!/usr/bin/python

# Import the Ansible Runner return data lib
from ansible.runner.return_data import ReturnData

# Define our ActionModule class (MUST BE NAMED ActionModule)
class ActionModule(object):

    # Define our Calss constructor method (Must be present)
    def __init__(self, runner):
        self.runner = runner

    # Define our run method (must be present)
    def run(self, conn, tmp, module_name, module_args, inject,
complex_args=None, **kwargs):
        return ReturnData(conn=conn, comm_ok=True,
result=dict(failed=False, changed=False, msg="Hello Ansible"))
```

So, as we can see, the plugin code simply adds functionality to the playbook by using a set of well-defined structured methods.

Callback plugins

Callback plugins in Ansible provide additional functionality to Ansible when responding to various events within the system. Callback plugins also control most of the execution output that is displayed when running a command-line program. In this section, we will take a look at callback plugins and learn how to implement additional callbacks within the Ansible subsystems.

The Python code for callback plugins must be stored in the `callback` folder, as we talked about earlier. The code that needs to be overridden by the class is shown as follows:

```python
#!/usr/bin/python

# Import CallbackPlugin base class
from ansible.plugins.callback import CallbackBase
from ansible import constants as C

# Define the CallBackModule class
class CallbackModule(CallbackBase):
    pass
```

The way Callback plugins work is similar to other plugins. They provide us with the ability to override various functionality developed within the initial Ansible implementation. Additional details on the specifics of overrides available can be found at `http://docs.ansible.com/ansible/dev_guide/developing_plugins.html`.

Connection plugins

Similar to callback and action plugins, connection plugins can also be added to enhance the capability of the Ansible subsystems. Out of the box, Ansible uses a `paramiko` SSH and a native SSH Protocol connection solution. In addition, there are some other minor libraries leveraged as well (`chroot`, `jail`, and so on.) These libraries can be leveraged via playbook's. It may become wanted to leverage an alternative connection type such as SNMP, or message for Ansible to use. It's really a simple procedure (for those with Python and programming knowledge) using the connection plugin option. To accomplish this, simply copy one of the formats of one of the existing connection types into a `plugins_connection` folder and modify it to suit your needs.

> Documentation for this plugin type is not comprehensive, and it is not available publicly yet by the Ansible creators. As such, it's recommended that you take a look at the Ansible source code for the existing connection plugins, for example. These examples can be found at `https://github.com/ansible/ansible/tree/devel/lib/ansible/plugins/connection`.

Lookup plugins

In this section, we will take a closer look at lookup plugins and learn what they are, where some examples can be found, and how to leverage them. To begin, let's better understand what a lookup plugin actually is. A lookup plugin is designed to retrieve information and datasets from external data sources. For example, the concept of Ansible iterations is developed using lookup plugins. More specifically, `with_fileglob` and `with_items` were implemented using the lookup plugin constructs.

Let's take a look at how to implement a look-up plugin based on the official Ansible source code documentation:

```
# This Code Example Comes from the Official Ansible Documentation Set
(http://www.ansible.com/)

from ansible.errors import AnsibleError, AnsibleParserError
from ansible.plugins.lookup import LookupBase
```

```
try:
    from __main__ import display
except ImportError:
    from ansible.utils.display import Display
    display = Display()

# This is the standard class for the LookupModule implementation it is
required to be this name
class LookupModule(LookupBase):

    # As with all our other plugins, the run method MUST be there
    def run(self, terms, variables=None, **kwargs):

        ret = []
        # Perform iteration
        for term in terms:

            display.debug("File lookup term: %s" % term)

            # Find the file in the expected search path
            lookupfile = self.find_file_in_search_path(variables, 'files',
term)
            display.vvvv(u"File lookup using %s as file" % lookupfile)
            try:
                if lookupfile:
                    contents, show_data =
self._loader._get_file_contents(lookupfile)
                    ret.append(contents.rstrip())
                else:
                    raise AnsibleParserError()

            except AnsibleParserError:
                raise AnsibleError("could not locate file in lookup: %s" %
term)
        return ret
```

This is an example of how this lookup is called:

```
---
- hosts: all
  vars:
  contents: "{{ lookup('file', '/etc/foo.txt') }}"
  tasks:

    - debug: msg="the value of foo.txt is {{ contents }} as seen today {{
lookup('pipe', 'date +"%Y-%m-%d"') }}"
```

Distributing Ansible plugins

We discussed this in some detail within each section of this chapter, but it deserves reiterating. The most effective way to enable and distribute an Ansible plugin is to create a subdirectory alongside the playbook, which will leverage the plugin, that is, to create one of the following directories along side your playbook:

- ./action_plugins
- ./lookup_plugins
- ./callback_plugins
- ./connection_plugins
- ./filter_plugins
- ./strategy_plugins
- ./cache_plugins
- ./test_plugins
- ./shell_plugins

In addition to this methodology for the distribution of a plugin, we could also use RPM or PIP to package the plugin and distribute it to the proper Ansible installation directory. The traditional installation location is set in the /etc/ansible/ansible.cfg file and can be altered as required.

Summary

In this chapter, we talked about extending Ansible. You learned that there are two types of extensions for Ansible. The first is an Ansible module, and the second one is an Ansible plugin. Ansible modules provide developers with the ability to add functionality to Ansible running on target hosts, whereas plugins extend the capabilities of the control server.

You learned how to set up a local development environment for both Ansible modules and Ansible plugins. Once we had the development environment taken care of, we looked at how to write modules using a Hello World example and how to extend Ansible with a new plugin that overrides functionality within the core Ansible plugin solution.

After that, we explored the plugin architecture and learned the various extension points that can be leveraged. This included action plugins, controller plugins, var plugins, and more.

In the next and final chapter, we will take a look at Ansible Galaxy. Ansible Galaxy is a user-managed distribution point for Ansible playbooks. It is a critical implementation for Ansible developers and makes the job of creating playbooks to perform common tasks a breeze. Let's get moving.

12
Ansible Galaxy

At this point in the book, we should have a pretty solid grasp of DevOps and Ansible and how to effectively implement DevOps patterns and organizational strategies using Ansible 2. From here, we will take a look at community resources provided by Ansible (Ansible Galaxy) and discover how to tap into a wealth of open source community-provided Ansible roles and playbook's.

Ansible's implementation has managed to standardize itself over the years and has become one of the leading DevOps Configuration Management, automation, and delivery solutions in the market. Ansible's success is primarily due to the modularity that is inherent in Ansible, its extensibility, Ansible Tower, and its community-supported Ansible Galaxy solution.

For those unaware of Ansible Galaxy, it is a robust and highly adaptable solution by which community members and playbook developers can create and share Ansible roles. This community-developed sharing solution provides a wealth of automation solutions for the community to partake in.

In this final chapter, we are going to take a look at Ansible's flagship playbook and role distribution solution: The Ansible Galaxy. We are going to explore how to leverage this innovative implementation to retrieve and submit role developments. We are going to explore how this solution works and learn how to make the best use of it.

The topics we are going to explore specifically include the following:

- Ansible Galaxy Fundamentals
- Understanding the command-line options available within Ansible Galaxy
- Understanding how to install roles onto your system using Ansible Galaxy
- Describing how to create and share with Ansible Galaxy

Ansible Galaxy Fundamentals

In this section, we are going to take a look at the Ansible Galaxy. We are going to explore what Ansible Galaxy is and how it works. To begin, let's define what Ansible Galaxy is. Ansible Galaxy is a website supported by a command-line interface, which provides an area for *role* and *playbook* developers to share and consume their creations. Each entry point into Ansible Galaxy is available independently and allows the community to leverage it as they see fit.

The Ansible Galaxy website

The Ansible Galaxy website is an Ansible-owned and community-supported role and playbook sharing solution. The Ansible Galaxy website hosts thousands of community-created roles and playbooks. The developers of these roles have created them in order to allow others to benefit from their efforts and leverage them to perform automated deployment and configuration management tasks.

At this point, it's a good idea to take a look at the Ansible Galaxy website. The Ansible Galaxy website and community is located at `https://galaxy.ansible.com/`.

The Ansible Galaxy website should look something like what is shown in the following screenshot:

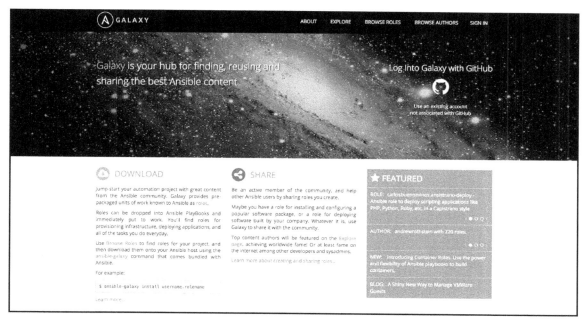

As we can see, the Ansible Galaxy website is broken down into a few distinct menu options. These subsections (highlighted at the top of the site) are as follows:

- **ABOUT**
- **EXPLORE**
- **BROWSE ROLES**
- **BROWSE AUTHORS**

Let's take a minute to briefly describe each of these sections and their role in the Ansible Galaxy universe:

- **ABOUT**: This section of the site provides some critical information related to Ansible Galaxy. This includes some basic tutorials on how to download roles one by one, how to download multiple roles at a time, advanced download options, how to create and share roles, best practices, automated testing techniques, and where to go if you have any questions.
- **EXPLORE**: The explore section provides us with a set of tagged criteria we can browse roles with. These tagged criteria allow us to look at roles available within Ansible Galaxy via the author name, most downloaded, most watched, and more.

- **BROWSE ROLES**: Browse roles are exactly what it sounds like; a role browser and search utility. This is probably the most used section of the website as it allows us to find and grab Ansible roles.
- **BROWSE AUTHORS**: Browse authors are a way for us to search through Ansible Galaxy and find roles created by specific people. This can be especially handy when searching for roles created by someone you know or a popular author.

In addition to the Ansible Galaxy main website, you can refer to the `https://www.ansible.com/` official documentation as well in relation to Ansible Galaxy help. The link for this documentation is `http://docs.ansible.com/ansible/galaxy.html`.

In addition to connecting to the central Ansible Galaxy website, you can can also run your own dedicated and private Ansible Galaxy server. This is because just like Ansible, Ansible Galaxy is also open source. More information on setting up a personal Ansible Galaxy server can be found at `https://github.com/ansible/galaxy`.

As you explore the Ansible Galaxy website, there are some important things to make note of when searching and using Ansible roles within a given system. These include the following:

- The role name
- Compatible platforms
- The installation command

Ansible Galaxy website is kind enough to provide us with the command-line solution for each given role. For example, the following screenshot provides a glimpse of how the Ansible Galaxy website outlines the role information for MySQL:

And once you click on the preferred role (in our case, it's **mysql**), we should see something like what is shown in the following screenshot:

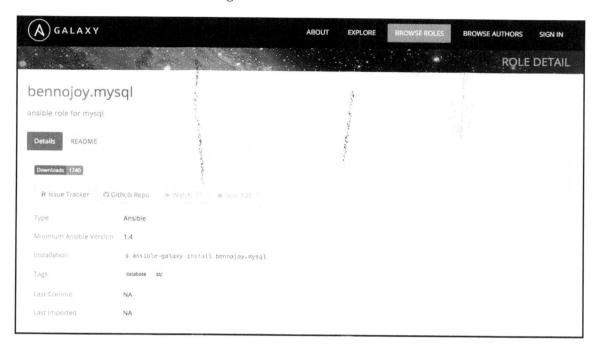

The Ansible Galaxy command-line interface

The Ansible Galaxy command-line interface is provided to users so they can automate the procurement of Ansible roles from the Ansible Galaxy website. This is a highly useful command-line tool, and we will be using it for the remainder of this chapter. To begin, we will want to verify that the Ansible Galaxy command-line tool is installed and functioning properly. Let's try the following command:

```
#> ansible-galaxy --help
```

The output of this command should be something like the following:

```
jmcallister@ubuntu:~$ sudo ansible-galaxy --help
Usage: ansible-galaxy [delete|import|info|init|install|list|login|remove|search|setup] [--help] [opt
ions] ...

Options:
  -h, --help      show this help message and exit
  -v, --verbose   verbose mode (-vvv for more, -vvvv to enable connection
                  debugging)
  --version       show program's version number and exit
ERROR! Missing required action
jmcallister@ubuntu:~$
```

Now that we have the pleasantries of how to basically invoke Ansible Galaxy out of the way, we can begin looking at the command-line switches available to the Ansible Galaxy solution.

The complete syntax for the `ansible-galaxy` installation (used to install roles on your system, login, and do much more) would look something like the following:

```
#> ansible-galaxy [ACTION] [options] [-r FILE | role_name(s)[,version] |
tar_file(s)]
```

If this looks slightly confusing, it's OK; it won't shortly. Next, we are going to go through the more important `ansible-galaxy` command-line options and you will learn how to use them in greater detail.

Ansible Galaxy command-line options explained

In this section, we are going to take a much closer look at the Ansible Galaxy command-line options and available parameters. The goal will be to really dive into the command line and better understand how the command-line implementation of Ansible Galaxy can make the Ansible administrators' life easier. We just looked (earlier) at an example of the complete syntax of the `ansible-galaxy` command. When using Ansible Galaxy, in the `ansible-galaxy` command, the formatting is <OPTION> followed by [PARAMS]. This is shown here:

```
#> ansible-galaxy <OPTION> [PARAMS]
```

So in all reality, the `<OPTION>` tag could be any of the following options:

```
[delete|import|info|init|install|list|login|remove|search|setup] [--help]
```

On the other hand, the `[PARAMS]` would be any of the option supported sub-arguments. Let's take a look at the primary options available to the `ansible-galaxy` command and see what each of these do and take a look at each option's available sub-arguments.

The install subcommand

The `install` subcommand is used by Ansible to install roles onto the control server. The general usage of this command is as follows:

```
ansible-galaxy install [options] [-r FILE | role_name(s)[,version] |
tar_file(s)]
```

A more realistic example of this command in action might be something like the following:

`ansible-galaxy install ANXS.postgresql`

As we saw earlier, the Ansible Galaxy website will provide us with the command-line syntax to install a given role, and as we can see, this is generally fairly straightforward.

The `install` option provides several options to install roles. These are described next:

- Using `username.role[,version]`: This solution offers us the ability to install a given role that we found within the Ansible Galaxy website. The syntax of this solution based on our previous `install` command example allows us to specify, say, `ansible-galaxy install ANXS.postgresql`, where `ANXS` is the username and `postgresql` is the role.
- Using a `filename -r-` option: This solution offers us the ability to install any number of roles provided within a text file. The text file would have one role per line with the same formatting requirements as the preceding option on each line:

  ```
  username.role[,version]
  ```

- Using a tarball: This option allows us to grab a role from another source (say, GitHub) and install the role by pointing Ansible Galaxy at the `tar.gz` file.

- Available options:
    - −f, −−force: Forces the overwriting of an existing role on the system.
    - −i, −−ignore-errors: This option ignores errors and allows Ansible Galaxy to continue with the next specified role.
    - −n, −−no-deps: This option removes the dependencies from the context of the ansible-galaxy command. This means that no dependencies will be installed along with the specified role.
    - −p ROLES_PATH, −−roles-path=ROLES_PATH: This optional path parameter, allows us to override the directory containing roles. Specifically it allows us to specify an alternate location for Galaxy to download them to. The default implementation for roles_path configured in the ansible.cfg file (/etc/ansible/roles if not configured).
    - −r ROLE_FILE, −−role-file=ROLE_FILE: A file containing a list of roles to be imported, as previously specified. This option cannot be used if a role name or .tar.gz have been specified.

The delete subcommand

The delete command option in Ansible Galaxy will remove a role from the galaxy.ansible.com registry. It is important to note that order to effectively remove a role, you will first need to authenticate using the login option. Some examples of how to use the DELETE option are provided next:

```
#> ansible-galaxy delete USER.ROLE
```

Available parameters are as follows:

- −c, −−ignore-certs: This specific option tells Ansible Galaxy to ignore TLS certificate errors.
- −s, −−server: This option overrides the default server https://galaxy.ansible.com. This is particularly useful when setting up your own Ansible Galaxy server.

The import subcommand

This `ansible-galaxy` option allows us to import a role from GitHub into the `galaxy.ansible.com` library. In order for this import solution to work, it will require user authentication with `galaxy.ansible.com` using the login subcommand. Let's take a look at how to use the `import` subcommand to import a role.

```
$> ansible-galaxy import [options] github_user github_repo
```

Available parameters are as follows:

- `-c, --ignore-certs`: This command-line option tells Ansible Galaxy to ignore SSL certs. The switch also ignores TLS certificate errors.
- `-s, --server`: Overrides the default server `https://galaxy.ansible.com`.
- `--branch`: This option lets us specify a specific branch to import into Ansible Galaxy. If a specific branch is not defined, the branch found in `meta/main.yml` is used.

The ifo subcommand

The `ansible-galaxy info` subcommand provides a detailed set of information related to a specific role. The results returned for the role include information from both the remote *Ansible Galaxy copy* and the *local copy*. An example of how to use the `info` subcommand is provided next:

```
$> ansible-galaxy info [options] role_name[, version]
```

Available options are as follows:

- `-p ROLES_PATH, --roles-path=ROLES_PATH`: The `roles-path` option provides us with the ability to specify a path to the directory containing our Ansible roles. The default location for roles is the `ROLES_PATH` specified in the `ansible.cfg` file (`/etc/ansible/roles` if not configured).
- `-c, --ignore-certs`: This ignores TLS certificate errors.
- `-s, --server`: This option overrides the default server `https://galaxy.ansible.com` and allows us to specify an alternate one.

The init command

The `init` command is used to initialize an empty role structure that could then be uploaded to `https://galaxy.ansible.com/`. This is a good way to begin Ansible Galaxy role development and is the preferred way to get started in creating the structures needed to begin development. The following is a syntax example of how to use the `init` command:

```
$> ansible-galaxy init [options] role_name
```

Available options are as follows:

- `-f, --force`: This option forces the `init` structure to automatically overwrite any existing roles in the path.
- `-p INIT_PATH, --init-path=INIT_PATH`: This option allows us to specify the path where the skeleton of the new role will be created. The default value for this is the current working directory.
- `--offline`: This option tells the `init` sub-argument to not query the `galaxy` API when creating roles.

The list subcommand

The `list` subcommand instructs Ansible Galaxy to show what roles are currently installed on the system. Through this command, we can also specify just the role name, and if it's actually installed, only that role will be shown. Let's take a look at an example of how to use this subcommand:

```
$> ansible-galaxy list [role_name]
```

Available options are `-p ROLES_PATH, --roles-path=ROLES_PATH`; this path allows us to specify the path to the directory containing our roles. The default value for this option is `roles_path`, which is traditionally configured in the `ansible.cfg` file located at `/etc/ansible/roles`.

The login subcommand

The Ansible Galaxy `login` subcommand provides us with the ability to authenticate between `ansible-galaxy` and the local command-line client. This authentication is particularly useful when uploading roles to Ansible Galaxy. Its also useful for importing roles into Ansible Galaxy from GitHub. In these cases (and a couple of others), the `login` command sequence is required before the operation can be performed. Let's take a look at the command-line syntax for the `login` subcommand:

```
$> ansible-galaxy login [options]
```

Available options are as follows:

- `-c, --ignore-certs`: This option ignores any TLS cert errors that may occur.
- `-s, --server`: This option tells Ansible Galaxy to override the default server `https://galaxy.ansible.com`.
- `--github-token`: If we don't wish to use our GitHub password, or if for your specific GitHub account two-factor authentication has been enabled, we can optionally use the `--github-token` parameter to pass a personal access token to the GitHub login solution. It is important to remember that this should be used only *if* we have two-factor authentication enabled on the GitHub account.

The remove subcommand

In this subsection, we are going to look at the `remove` subcommand for Ansible Galaxy. This specific subcommand is used to remove one or more roles. Let's take a quick look at an example of the syntax usage for this command:

```
$> ansible-galaxy remove rolea roleb ...
```

Available options are `-p ROLES_PATH, --roles-path=ROLES_PATH`; this path allows us to specify the path to the directory containing our roles. The default value for this option is `ROLES_PATH`, which is traditionally configured in the `ansible.cfg` file located at `/etc/ansible/roles`.

The search subcommand

The Ansible Galaxy solution has a really handy `search` subcommand. This subcommand provides us with the ability to search for specific roles on the Ansible Galaxy server. In addition to basic search functionality, we can also search and filter the results. Let's take a minute to look at the syntax of this useful feature:

```
$> ansible-galaxy search [options] [searchtermZ searchtermA]
```

Available options are as follows:

- `--galaxy-tags`: The `tags` option provides a **Comma Separated Value (CSV)** list of the tags that we want the Galaxy server to filter.
- `--platforms`: This option allows us to filter roles based on the platforms supported. To use it, we will need to provide a comma-separated list of platforms on which to filter.

- `--author`: This option allows us to specify the username we want to filter by.
- `-c, --ignore-certs`: This ignores TLS certificate errors.
- `-s, --server`: This option allows us to change the server URL of Ansible Galaxy. For example, this might be useful if we run our own Ansible Galaxy server.

The setup subcommand

The `setup` action allows Ansible Galaxy to integrate with Travis CI. This, in turn, will allow Ansible Galaxy to receive notifications from Travis CI upon completion of the build. It is important to note that prior to being able to use this integration, Ansible Galaxy must first be authenticated with the `galaxy.ansible.com` library.

An example of how to use the `setup` command is provided next:

```
$ ansible-galaxy setup [options] source github_user github_repo secret
```

The help command

This command-line option displays a brief help message and exits. An example of the output from the `help` command is provided next:

```
jmcallister@ubuntu:~$ sudo ansible-galaxy --help
Usage: ansible-galaxy [delete|import|info|init|install|list|login|remove|search|setup] [--help] [opt
ions] ...

Options:
  -h, --help      show this help message and exit
  -v, --verbose   verbose mode (-vvv for more, -vvvv to enable connection
                  debugging)
  --version       show program's version number and exit
ERROR! Missing required action
jmcallister@ubuntu:~$
```

Summary

In this final chapter, we took a look at how to use Ansible Galaxy. Ansible Galaxy is a really useful solution in sharing and communicating Ansible roles. This solution can take a lot of the guess work out of Ansible. Generally, there is a saying within the Ansible Galaxy community: "There's a galaxy role for that", and indeed, there probably is.

As we wrap up our journey through DevOps and Ansible, it's important to remember that implementing DevOps can be a tough challenge for any organization. There are a lot of people who will need to work in concert to develop a unified process, a set of rigid standards while maintaining a flexible atmosphere that technology demands.

In your quest to implement DevOps with Ansible 2, Ansible provides a much-needed automation platform and glue within an organization that can be leveraged as a foundational point for future DevOps-oriented improvements. It is my hope as the author of this book that the knowledge contained within proves to be useful for your organization and that your DevOps implementations are successful.

Index

www.ingramcontent.com/pod-product-compliance
Lightning Source LLC
Chambersburg PA
CBHW060534060326

40690CB00017B/3481